George A. Hubbell

The Chapel Hymn Book

containing over four hundred hymns and spiritual songs

George A. Hubbell

The Chapel Hymn Book
containing over four hundred hymns and spiritual songs

ISBN/EAN: 9783337180577

Printed in Europe, USA, Canada, Australia, Japan

Cover: Foto ©Thomas Meinert / pixelio.de

More available books at **www.hansebooks.com**

THE CHAPEL HYMN BOOK:

CONTAINING OVER FOUR HUNDRED

Hymns and Spiritual Songs;

WITH THE

First Strain of the Melody prefixed to the Hymns;

DESIGNED FOR USE IN

PRAYER MEETINGS, REVIVALS, Etc.

COMPILED BY REV. GEO. A. HUBBELL.

"Singing and making melody in your heart to the Lord."—*Paul.*

NEW YORK:
N. TIBBALS & CO., 37 PARK ROW.

1868.

Entered according to Act of Congress in the year 1868,
By TIBBALS & CO.,
In the Clerk's Office of the District Court of the United States, for the Southern District of New York.

PREFATORIAL.

This Hymn-Book has grown out of a sense of want, increasingly felt through a pastorate of over twenty years;—the want of appropriate singing in social meetings for devotion.

The church hymn-books, though containing the richest spiritual poetry, have too much of stateliness; they are too didactic, too deficient in those lively sentimental hymns and choruses which thrill the popular heart. The use of these books in social meetings fosters a stiffness, formality and coldness, which tend to make the Chapel an uninteresting and unpopular place. Moreover, these books are either too large, or are in such small type, that few persons will carry them to the prayer-meeting: hence, either but a small portion of the congregation sing at all; or hymns familiar to the people will be sung from week to week, through years of wearisome repetitions, until all interest in this part of Divine worship has ceased.

The want of a suitable collection of prayer-meeting hymns, has opened the way for the introduction of many light, frivolous pieces in some congregations, which has inspired a piety as vapid and superficial as the doggerel songs that produced it. To meet the want so generally felt, many little volumes, of more or less merit, have been compiled; and, for a time, they have done good service. But, after examining near a score of these books, hoping to find one in all respects adapted to the wants of the Chapel, the writer has not been able to find one that he could fully recommend to his congregation for general and permanent use. Some of them are too large and unportable: others contain so much music that they too much restrict the number and variety of the hymns: in some the hymns are not classified so as to aid in finding, on the instant, just what is needed: many of them attempt too much — encumbering their pages with Sunday-school, temperance, patriotic and other hymns, that are not used in the Chapel; and other books are too small.

This book has been compiled with the hope of approaching the golden mean between these various extremes. Its selections have been made from a very wide range—near ten thousand hymns having been gleaned from, and those have been selected which were deemed most spiritual and best adapted to Chapel use. The standard hymns of Wesley, Watts, Montgomery and Newton largely enrich these pages; while the best of those of more recent authorship, whose merits must secure for them a wide-spread popularity, and some of which have not yet appeared in the church and chapel hymn-books, are here given. Over four hundred of these choice and approved hymns are here brought together in a neat, portable volume, and arranged under the appropriate captions of Invocation, Awakening, Inviting, Penitence, Faith and Assurance, Joy and Praise, The Christian Life, Consecration and Holiness, The Final Triumph and Home in Heaven. These captions are so conspicuously printed that, on opening the book at random, the reader will instantly see the class of subjects to which the hyms before him belong. Much labor has been spent in so arranging the hymns, that no leaves have to be turned while singing any one piece. The *tunes* selected are the most popular and familiar ones in general use. Only enough of each tune is published to enable the Precentor to give it the right pitch, time and movement. The first strain of the air is sufficient to call up the whole tune, in all its parts.

Extensive correspondence with the authors and owners of the copyrights of these hymns has been had, and their consent to this use of them has been obtained. Nevertheless, some are here published anonymously—just as we found them. Acknowledgements are hereby gratefully tendered to Messrs. Perkinpine & Higgins, (Phila.) Publishers of Revival and Camp-Meeting Minstrel; to Mr. Wm. B. Bradbury, New York, the author of the Golden Chain, Golden Censor, and several other exquisite Sunday-school books; to Hon. Samuel Booth, Brooklyn, Compiler of Sunday-school Hymns; to H. Waters, Publisher of Sunday-school Bell, New York; and to Dr. H. Mattison, Compiler of Sacred Melodies, for permission to use hymns in their collections; also to others, whose names appear in connection with their valuable contributions to this work.

G. A. H.

BROOKLYN, January, 1868.

CONTENTS.

		Pages.
I.	Invocation	1- 27
II.	Awakening	28- 51
III.	Inviting to Jesus	52- 75
IV.	Penitently Seeking God	76-103
V.	Faith and Assurance	104-139
VI.	Joy and Praise	135-174
VII.	The Christian Life	180-231
VIII.	Consecration & Holiness	232-277
IX.	The Triumph and Home in Heaven	278-319
X.	Closing Hymns and Doxology	320-324

CHAPEL HYMNS.

I.—INVOCATION.

GIVE.   C. M.

1
COME, Holy Ghost, inspire our songs
  With thine immortal flame;
Enlarge our hearts, unloose our tongues,
  To praise the Saviour's name.

2 How great the riches of his grace!
  He left his throne above,
And, swift to save our ruin'd race,
  He flew on wings of love.

3 Now pardon, life and joys divine,
  In rich abundance flow,
For guilty rebels, dead in sin,
  And doom'd to endless wo.

4 The' almighty Former of the skies
  Stoop'd to our low abode;
While angels view'd with wond'ring eyes,
  And hail'd the' incarnate God.

5 Renew our souls with heavenly strength,
  That we may fully prove   [length,
The height, and depth, and breadth, and
  Of such transcendent love.

INVOCATION.

HENDON. 5th P. M.

2

COME, my soul, thy suit prepare;
Jesus loves to answer prayer;
He himself invites thee near,
Bids thee ask him, waits to hear.

2 Lord, I come to thee for rest;
Take possession of my breast;
There thy blood-bought right maintain,
And without a rival reign.

3 While I am a pilgrim here,
Let thy love my spirit cheer;
As my guide, my guard, my friend,
Lead me to my journey's end.

4 Show me what I have to do;
Every hour my strength renew;
Let me live a life of faith;
Let me die thy people's death.

NEWTON.

3

LORD, we come before thee now,
At thy feet we humbly bow;
O, do not our suit disdain;
Shall we seek thee, Lord, in vain?

2 Lord, on thee our souls depend;
In compassion now descend;
Fill our hearts with thy rich grace,
Tune our lips to sing thy praise.

3 Comfort those who weep and mourn;
  Let the time of joy return;
  Those that are cast down lift up;
  Make them strong in faith and hope.

4 Grant that all may seek and find
  Thee, a gracious God and kind:
  Heal the sick, the captive free;
  Let us all rejoice in thee.

HAMMOND.

WILMOT. 5th P. M.

4.

SON of God, thy blessing grant;
  Still supply my every want;
  Tree of life, thine influence shed:
  From thy fulness I am fed.

2 Tend'rest branch, alas! am I,—
  Wither without thee, and die;
  Weak as helpless infancy:
  O confirm my soul in thee!

3 Unsustained by thee, I fall:
  Send the help for which I call;
  Weaker than a bruised reed,
  Help I every moment need.

4 All my hopes on thee depend;
  Love me, save me to the end;
  Give me persevering grace;
  Take the everlasting praise.

C. WESLEY.

INVOCATION.

RETREAT. L. M.

5

FROM every stormy wind that blows,
  From every swelling tide of woes,
There is a calm, a sure retreat:
'Tis found beneath the mercy-seat.

2 There is a place where Jesus sheds
The oil of gladness on our heads;
A place than all beside more sweet, -
It is the blood-bought mercy-seat.

3 Ah! whither could we flee for aid,
When tempted, desolate, dismay'd?
Or how the hosts of hell defeat,
Had suff'ring saints no mercy-seat?

4 There, there on eagles' wings we soar,
And sin and sense molest no more; [greet,
And Heaven comes down our souls to
While glory crowns the mercy-seat.
STOWELL.

6

PRAYER is appointed to convey
  The blessings God designs to give;
Long as they live should Christians pray;
  They learn to pray when first they live.

2 If pain afflict, or wrongs oppress;
  If cares distract, or fears dismay;
If guilt deject; if sin distress;
  In every case, still watch and pray.

3 'Tis prayer supports the soul that's weak;
　　Though thought be broken, language lame,
Pray, if thou canst or canst not speak;
　　But pray with faith in Jesus' name.

4 Depend on him; thou canst not fail;
　　Make all thy wants and wishes known;
Fear not; his merits must prevail;
　　Ask but in faith, it shall be done.

HART.

Duke Street.   L. M.

7

O THOU, our Saviour, Brother, Friend,
　　Behold a cloud of incense rise;
The prayers of saints to heaven ascend,
　　Grateful, accepted sacrifice.

2 Regard our prayers for Zion's peace;
　　Shed in our hearts thy love abroad;
Thy gifts abundantly increase;
　　Enlarge, and fill us all with God.

3 Before thy sheep, great Shepherd, go,
　　And guide into thy perfect will:
Cause us thy hallow'd name to know;
　　The work of faith in us fulfill.

4 Help us to make our calling sure;
　　O let us all be saints indeed,
And pure, as thou thyself art pure,—
　　Conform'd in all things to our Head.

C. WESLEY.

INVOCATION.

SWEET HOUR OF PRAYER. L. M. D.

Golden Chain. By permission of W. B. Bradbury.

1 SWEET hour of prayer! sweet hour of prayer!
  That calls me from this world of care,
  And bids me at my Father's throne
  Make all my wants and wishes known.
  In seasons of distress and grief,
  My soul has often found relief;
  And oft escaped the tempest's snare,
  By thy return, sweet hour of prayer.

2 Sweet hour of prayer! sweet hour of prayer!
  Thy wings shall my petitions bear,
  To him whose truth and faithfulness
  Engage the waiting soul to bless.
  And, since he bids me seek his face,
  Believe his word and trust his grace,
  I'll cast on him my every care,
  And wait for thee, sweet hour of prayer.

3 Sweet hour of prayer! sweet hour of prayer!
  May I thy consolation share,
  Till, from Mount Pisgah's lofty height,
  I view my home and take my flight.
  This robe of flesh I'll drop, and rise,
  To seize the everlasting prize;
  And shout, while passing through the air,
  Farewell, farewell, sweet hour of prayer.

INVOCATION. 13

MARTYN. 7th P. M.

9

SAVIOUR, when, in dust, to thee
Low we bow the adoring knee,—
When, repentant, to the skies
Scarce we lift our streaming eyes,—
O, by all thy pain and wo
Suffer'd once for man below,
Bending from thy throne on high,
Hear us when to thee we cry.

2 By thine hour of dark despair,
By thine agony of prayer;
By the cross, the nail, the thorn,
Piercing spear, and tort'ring scorn
By the gloom that veil'd the skies
O'er the dreadful sacrifice,—
Jesus, look with pitying eye;
Listen to our humble cry.

3 By the deep, expiring groan;
By the sad, sepulchral stone;
By the vault whose dark abode
Held in vain the rising God,—
O, from earth to heaven restored,
Mighty, re-ascended Lord,
Saviour, Prince, exalted high,
Hear, O hear, our humble cry.

GLENELG.

INVOCATION.

BALERMA.　　　　　　　　　C. M.

10

LORD! when we bend before thy throne,
　And our confessions pour,
O may we feel the sins we own,
　And hate what we deplore.

2 Our contrite spirits pitying see:
　True penitence impart;
And let a healing ray from thee,
　Beam peace into each heart.

3 When we disclose our wants in prayer,
　O let our wills resign;
And not a thought our bosom share,
　Which is not wholly thine.

4 And when with heart and voice we strive
　Our grateful hymns to raise,
Let love divine within us live,
　And fill our souls with praise.

11

ETERNAL Spirit! God of truth!
　Our contrite hearts inspire;
Kindle a flame of heavenly love—
　The pure celestial fire.

2 Subdue the power of every sin,
　Whate'er that sin may be;
That we, in singleness of heart,
　May worship only thee.

3 Then with our spirits witness bear,
   That we are sons of God;
Redeem'd from sin, and death, and hell,
   Through Christ's atoning blood.

MEAR.   C. M.

12
FATHER, behold, with gracious eyes,
   The souls before thy throne,
Who now present their sacrifice,
   And seek thee in thy Son.

2 Well pleased in him thyself declare
   Thy pard'ning love reveal;
The peaceful answer of our prayer,
   On every conscience seal.

3 On me, on all, some gift bestow,
   Some blessing now impart;
The seed of life eternal sow,
   In every waiting heart.

4 Refresh us with a ceaseless shower
   Of graces from above,
Till all receive the perfect power
   Of everlasting love.

                                    C. WESLEY.

INVOCATION.

KENTUCKY. S. M.

13

THE praying spirit breathe;
  The watching power impart;
From all entanglements beneath,
  Call off my peaceful heart.

2 My feeble mind sustain,
  By worldly thoughts oppress'd;
Appear, and bid me turn again
  To my eternal rest.

3 Swift to my rescue come;
  Thine own this moment seize;
Gather my wand'ring spirit home,
  And keep in perfect peace.

4 Suffer'd no more to rove
  O'er all the earth abroad,
Arrest the pris'ner of thy love,
  And shut me up in God.

C. WESLEY.

14

JESUS, we look to thee,
  Thy promised presence claim;
Thou in the midst of us shalt be,
  Assembled in thy name.

2 Not in the name of pride
  Or selfishness we meet;
From nature's paths we turn aside,
  And worldly thoughts forget.

3 We meet the grace to take,
 Which thou hast freely given;
 We meet on earth for thy dear sake,
 That we may meet in heaven.

4 Present we know thou art,
 But O, thyself reveal!
 Now, Lord, let every bounding heart
 Thy mighty comfort feel.

C. WESLEY.

AYLESBURY. S. M.

15

O LORD, thy work revive,
 In Zion's gloomy hour,
And let our dying graces live
 By thy restoring power.

2 O let thy chosen few
 Awake to earnest prayer;
Their covenant again renew,
 And walk in filial fear.

3 Thy Spirit then will speak
 Through lips of humble clay,
Till hearts of adamant shall break,—
 Till rebels shall obey.

4 Now lend thy gracious ear;
 Now listen to our cry;
O come, and bring salvation near;
 Our souls on thee rely.

HASTINGS.

INVOCATION.

OLMUTZ. S. M.

16

BEFORE thy throne we bow,
  O thou almighty King;
Here we present the solemn vow,
  And hymns of praise we sing.

2 While in thy house we kneel,
    With trust and holy fear,
  Thy mercy and thy truth reveal,
    And lend a gracious ear.

3 Lord, teach our hearts to pray,
    And tune our lips to sing;
  Nor from thy presence cast away
    The sacrifice we bring.

JERVIS.

17

LORD God, the Holy Ghost!
  In this accepted hour,
As on the day of Pentecost,
  Descend in all thy power.

2 We meet with one accord
    In our appointed place,
  And wait the promise of our Lord,—
    The Spirit of all grace.

3 Like mighty rushing wind
    Upon the waves beneath,
  Move with one impulse every mind;
    One soul, one feeling breathe.

INVOCATION.

4 The young, the old inspire
    With wisdom from above;
And give us hearts and tongues of fire,
    To pray, and praise, and love.
                                    MONTGOMERY.

CARMARTHEN.   3d P. M.

18

O THOU that hearest prayer,
    Attend our humble cry;
And let thy servants share
    Thy blessing from on high:
We plead the promise of thy word;—
Grant us thy Holy Spirit, Lord!

2 If earthly parents hear
    Their children when they cry;
If they, with love sincere,
    Their children's wants supply;
Much more wilt thou thy love display,
And answer when thy children pray.

3 Our heavenly Father, thou;
    We, children of thy grace;
O let thy spirit now
    Descend and fill the place;
That all may feel the heavenly flame,
And all unite to praise thy name.

INVOCATION.

AMERICA.   19th P. M.

19

C OME, thou Almighty King,
  Help us thy Name to sing,
    Help us to praise:
Father all-glorious,
O'er all victorious,
Come, and reign over us,
    Ancient of days.

2 Come, thou incarnate Word,
  Gird on thy mighty sword,
    Our prayer attend;
Come, and thy people bless,
And give thy word success:
Spirit of holiness,
    On us descend.

3 Come, holy Comforter,
  Thy sacred witness bear,
    In this glad hour:
Thou who Almighty art,
Now rule in every heart,
And ne'er from us depart,
    Spirit of power.

SWANWICK.   C. M.

20
SPIRIT of life, and light, and love,
　Thy heavenly influence give;
Quicken our souls, our guilt remove,
　That we in Christ may live.

2 To our benighted minds reveal
　　The glories of his grace,
And bring us where no clouds conceal
　　The brightness of his face.

3 His love within us shed abroad,—
　　Life's ever-springing well;
Till God in us, and we in God,
　　In love eternal dwell.
HUMPHRIES.

21
FATHER, to thee my soul I lift;
　My soul on thee depends;
Convinced that every perfect gift
　From thee alone descends.

2 Mercy and grace are thine alone,
　　And power and wisdom too;
Without the Spirit of thy Son,
　　We nothing good can do.

3 We cannot speak one useful word,
　　One holy thought conceive,
Unless, in answer to our Lord,
　　Thyself the blessing give.

4 His blood demands the purchased grace;
　　His blood's availing plea
Obtain'd the help for all our race,
　　And sends it down to me.
C WESLEY.

INVOCATION.

FOUNTAIN. C. M.

22

FOUNTAIN of life, to all below
  Let thy salvation roll;
Water, replenish, and o'erflow
  Every believing soul.

2 The well of life to us thou art,—
  Of joy, the swelling flood;
Wafted by thee, with willing heart,
  We swift return to God.

3 We soon shall reach the boundless sea;
  Into thy fulness fall;
Be lost and swallow'd up in thee,—
  Our God, our All in All.

C. WESLEY.

23

SEE, Jesus, thy disciples see;
  The promised blessing give;
Met in thy name, we look to thee,
  Expecting to receive.

2 Thee we expect, our faithful Lord,
  Who in thy name are join'd;
We wait, according to thy word,
  Thee in the midst to find.

3 With us thou art assembled here,
  But O, thyself reveal;
Son of the living God, appear!
  Let us thy presence feel.

4 Breathe on us, Lord, in this our day,
  And these dry bones shall live;
Speak peace into our hearts, and say,
  The Holy Ghost receive.
                              C. WESLEY.

ARLINGTON.   C. M.

24

PRAYER is the soul's sincere desire,
  Utter'd or unexpress'd;
The motion of a hidden fire
  That trembles in the breast.

2 Prayer is the simplest form of speech
    That infant lips can try;
  Prayer, the sublimest strains that reach
    The Majesty on high.

3 Prayer is the Christian's vital breath,
    The Christian's native air;
  His watchword at the gates of death,—
    He enters heaven with prayer.

4 Prayer is the contrite sinner's voice,
    Returning from his ways;
  While angels, in their songs, rejoice,
    And cry: Behold, he prays!

5 O Thou, by whom we come to God,—
    The Life, the Truth, the Way,—
  The path of prayer thyself hast trod:
    Lord, teach us how to pray!
                              MONTGOMERY.

INVOCATION.

PRAYER.   5th P. M.

25

GOD of Love, who hearest prayer,
  Kindly for thy people care,
Who on thee alone depend:
Love us, save us to the end.

2 Save us, in the prosp'rous hour,
From the flatt'ring tempter's power;
From his unsuspected wiles,—
From the world's pernicious smiles.

3 Never let the world break in;
Fix a mighty gulf between;
Keep us little and unknown,
Prized and loved by God alone.

4 Let us still to thee look up,—
Thee, thy Israel's strength and hope;
Nothing know, or seek, beside
Jesus, and him crucified.

C. WESLEY

26

FATHER, at thy footstool see
  Those who now are one in thee:
Draw us by thy grace alone:
Give, O give us to thy Son.

2 Jesus, Friend of human kind,
Let us in thy name be join'd;
Each to each unite and bless;
Keep us still in perfect peace.

3 Heavenly, all-alluring Dove,
  Shed thy overshadowing love;
  Love, the sealing grace, impart;
  Dwell within our single heart.

4 Father, Son, and Holy Ghost,
  Be to us what Adam lost;
  Let us in thine image rise;
  Give us back our Paradise.
                                C. WESLEY.

HEBRON.   L. M.

27

O THOU who camest from above,
  The pure celestial fire to' impart,
Kindle a flame of sacred love,
  On the mean altar of my heart.

2 There let it for thy glory burn,
    With inextinguishable blaze;
  And trembling to its Source return,
    In humble love and fervent praise.

3 Jesus, confirm my heart's desire,
    To work, and speak, and think for thee;
  Still let me guard the holy fire,
    And still stir up thy gift in me.

4 Ready for all thy perfect will,
    My acts of faith and love repeat,
  Till death thy endless mercies seal,
    And make the sacrifice complete.
                                C. WESLEY

INVOCATION.

SICILIAN HYMN. 9th P. M.

28

IN thy name, O Lord, assembling,
   We, thy people, now draw near:
Teach us to rejoice with trembling;
   Speak, and let thy servants hear:
      Hear with meekness,—
Hear thy word with godly fear.

2 While our days on earth are lengthen'd,
   May we give them, Lord, to thee:
Cheer'd by hope, and daily strengthen'd,
   May we run, nor weary be;
      Till thy glory,
Without cloud, in heaven we see.

3 There, in worship purer, sweeter,
   All thy people shall adore;
Sharing then in rapture greater
Than they could conceive before:—
      Full enjoyment,—
Full and pure, forever more.

4 Saints and angels, join'd in concert,
   Sing the praises of the Lamb;
While the blissful seats of heaven
   Sweetly echo with his name:
      Hallelujah!
Sinners here may do the same.

INVOCATION.

THE ROCK HIGHER THAN I. P. M.

29

IN seasons of grief, to my God I'll repair,
When my heart is o'erwhelm'd with sorrow and care,
From the ends of the earth, unto thee will I cry;
Lead me to the Rock that is higher than I.
      Higher than I, higher than I,
Lead me to the Rock that is higher than I.

2 When Satan, the tempter, comes in like a flood,
To drive my poor soul from the fountain of good,
I'll pray to the Lord, who for sinners did die—
Lead me to the Rock that is higher than I.
      Higher than I, higher than I,
Lead me to the Rock that is higher than I.

3 And when I have finish'd my pilgrimage here,
Complete in Christ's righteousness I shall appear;
In the swellings of Jordan all dangers defy,
And look to the Rock that is higher than I.
      Higher than I, higher than I,
And look to the Rock that is higher than I.

4 And when the last trumpet shall sound through the
And the dead from the dust of the earth shall arise, [skies,
Transported I'll join with the ransom'd on high
To praise the great Rock that is higher than I.
      Higher than I, higher than I,
'To praise the great Rock that is higher than I.

SACRED MELODIES, p. 321

II.—AWAKENING.

SHAWMUT. S. M.

30

AND canst thou, sinner, slight
  The call of love Divine?
Shall God with tenderness invite,
  And gain no thought of thine?

2 Wilt thou not cease to grieve
  The Spirit from thy breast,
Till he thy wretched soul shall leave,
  With all thy sins opprest?

3 To-day a pardoning God
  Will hear the suppliant pray;
To-day a Saviour's cleansing blood
  Will wash thy guilt away.

4 But grace so dearly bought,
  If yet thou wilt despise,   [fraught
Thy fearful doom, with vengeance
  Will fill thee with surprise.

HYDE.

31

THIS world can never give
  The bliss for which we sigh;
'Tis not the whole of life to live,
  Nor all of death to die.

2 Beyond this vale of tears
  There is a life above,
Unmeasured by the flight of years;
  And all that life is love.

3 There is a death, whose pang
    Outlasts the fleeting breath:
O! what eternal horrors hang
    Around the second death.

4 Thou God of truth and grace,
    Teach us that death to shun;
Lest we be banished from thy face,
    For evermore undone.

MONTGOMERY.

DITSON.   C. M.

32

SINNERS, this solemn truth regard—
    Hear, all ye sons of men,
For Christ the Saviour hath declared:
    "Ye must be born again."

2 Whate'er might be your birth or blood,
    A sinner's boast is vain;
Thus saith the glorious Son of God,
    "Ye must be born again."

3 Your nature totally depraved,
    Your heart a sink of sin;
Without a change you can't be saved;
    "Ye must be born again."

4 Spirit of life, thy grace impart,
    And breathe on sinners slain;
Bear witness, Lord, in every part,
    That we are born again."

CHANGED FROM HOSKINS.

AWAKENING.

HEDDING. 4th P. M.

33
1. AND am I only born to die?
And must I suddenly comply
With nature's stern decree?
What after death for me remains?
Celestial joys, or hellish pains,
To all eternity.

2 How then ought I on earth to live,
While God prolongs the kind reprieve,
And props the house of clay?
My sole concern, my single care,
To watch, and tremble, and prepare
Against that fatal day.

3 No room for mirth or trifling here—
For worldly hope or worldly fear,
If life so soon is gone;
If now the Judge is at the door,
And all mankind must stand before
The' inexorable throne!

4 No matter which my thoughts employ,
A moment's misery or joy;
But, O! when both shall end,
Where shall I find my destined place?
Shall I my everlasting days
With fiends or angels spend?

5 Nothing is worth a thought beneath,
But how I may escape the death
That never, never dies!

How make mine own election sure;
And when I fail on earth, secure
A mansion in the skies.   C. WESLEY.

AYLESBURY.   S. M.

34
AND am I born to die?
  To lay this body down?
And must my trembling spirit fly
  Into a world unknown?—
A land of deepest shade,
  Unpierced by human thought;
The dreary regions of the dead,
  Where all things are forgot!

2 Soon as from earth I go;
  What will become of me?
Eternal happiness or wo
  Must then my portion be:
Waked by the trumpet's sound,
  I from my grave shall rise,
And see the Judge with glory crown'd,
  And see the flaming skies!

3 How shall I leave my tomb—
  With triumph or regret?
A fearful or a joyful doom,
  A curse or blessing, meet?
Will angel bands convey
  Their brother to the bar?
Or devils drag my soul away,
  To meet its sentence there?   C. WESLEY.

AWAKENING.

WINDHAM. L. M.

35

BROAD is the road that leads to death,
And thousands walk together there;
But wisdom shows a narrow path,
With here and there a traveller.

2 "Deny thyself and take thy cross,"
Is the Redeemer's great command;
Nature must count her gold but dross,
If she would gain this heavenly land.

3 The fearful soul that tires and faints,
And walks the ways of God no more,
Is but esteemed almost a saint,
And makes his own destruction sure.

4 Lord, let not all my hopes be vain;
Create my heart entirely new;
Which hypocrites could ne'er attain—
Which base apostates never knew.

WATTS.

36

THE day of wrath, that dreadful day,
When heaven and earth shall pass away!
What power shall be the sinner's stay?
How shall he meet that dreadful day—

2 When, shriv'ling like a parched scroll,
The flaming heavens together roll;
And, louder yet, and yet more dread,
Swells the high trump that wakes the dead?

3 O, on that day, that wrathful day,
When man to judgment wakes from clay,
Be thou, O Christ, the sinner's stay,
Though heaven and earth shall pass away.
W. SCOTT.

37

WHILE God invites, how blest the day!
  How sweet the Gospel's charming sound!
Come, sinners, haste, O haste away,
  While yet a pard'ning God is found.

2 Soon, borne on time's most rapid wing,
  Shall death command you to the grave,—
Before his bar your spirits bring,
  And none be found to hear or save.

3 In that lone land of deep despair,
  No Sabbath's heavenly light shall rise,—
No God regard your bitter prayer,
  No Saviour call you to the skies.
DWIGHT.

38

WHERE are the dead?—In heaven or hell
  Their disembodied spirits dwell;
Their perish'd forms, in bonds of clay,
Reserved until the judgment-day.

2 Where are the living?—On the ground
Where prayer is heard and mercy found;
Where, in the compass of a span,
The mortal makes th' immortal man.

3 Then, timely warn'd let us begin
To follow Christ and flee from sin;
Daily grow up in him our Head,
Lord of the living and the dead.
MONTGOMERY.

AWAKENING.

PLEADING SAVIOUR.   8s. & 7s.

39

NOW the Saviour standeth pleading,
  At the sinner's bolted heart;
Now in heaven he's interceding,
  Undertaking sinner's part.

CHORUS.—
  Sinner, can you hate this Saviour?
  Will you thrust him from your arms?
  Once he died for your behaviour,
  Now he calls you by his charms.

2 See him bleeding, dying, rising,
    To prepare you heavenly rest;
  Listen, while he kindly calls you;
    Hear, and be for ever blest.

3 Sinner! hear your God and Saviour;
    Hear his gracious voice to-day;
  Turn from all your vain behavior;
    O, repent, return and pray!

4 Will you plunge in endless darkness,
    There to bear eternal pain?
  Or, to realms of glorious brightness,
    Rise, and with him ever reign?

5 Come, for all things now are ready:
    Yet there's room for many more;
  O ye blind, ye lame, and needy,
    Come to wisdom's boundless store.

AWAKENING.

NETTLETON.   9th P. M.

40

STOP, poor sinners, and look yonder!
  See your sins like mountains rise;
O, astonishing the number,
Higher mounting than the skies!
    Cry for mercy,
Dread the death that never dies!

2 On the crumbling banks of ruin,
How can you securely dwell?
Surely vengeance is pursuing,
And will sweep you down to hell!
    Then to heaven
Finally you'll bid farewell.

3 See how fast your time is flying!
Will ye sinners yet delay?
One is gone; another's dying;
O, to God for mercy pray!
    Time is precious;
God may call YOU next away.

4 Now's the time for preparation,
While the vital air you breathe;
God is offering you salvation,
Calls you yet to turn and live.
    Boundless mercy!
All who come he will receive.

                    R. & C. M. MINSTREL;
By permission of Perkinpine & Higgins, Phila.

AWAKENING.

BRATTLE STREET. C. M. D.

41

O SINNER, on the brink of death,
  Why plod thy toilsome way,
Along the slippery path of guilt,
  Without one cheering ray?
Shall love implore with tearful eye?
  Shall Jesus die in vain?
Stop, sinner, in thy mad career,
  Thou must be born again.

2 Where is thy trust beyond the grave?
    And where thy hope of Heaven?
  Thou hast no pardoning voice within
    To speak thy sins forgiven.
  Boast not thy merits or thy works,
    For both alike are vain;
  If thou would'st win eternal life,
    Thou must be born again.

3 Give God thy heart; a simple act
    He justly claims of thee;
  Repent, believe, and thou shalt find
    A pardon full and free.
  Behold the bleeding Lamb of God—
    The Lamb for sinner's slain;
  Whose law demands of every soul
    "Ye must be born again."

                              FANNY CROSBY

PETERBORO'. C. M.

42

ALMIGHTY God, thy piercing eye
  Strikes through the shades of night ;
And our most secret actions lie
  All open to thy sight.

2 There's not a sin that we commit,
  Nor wicked word we say,
But in thy dreadful book 'tis writ.
  Against the judgment-day.

3 Lord, at thy feet ashamed I lie,
  Upward I dare not look;
Pardon my sins before I die,
  And blot them from thy book.

43

THAT awful day will surely come,
  The' appointed hour makes haste,
When I must stand before my Judge,
  And pass the solemn test.

2 Jesus, thou source of all my joys,—
  Thou ruler of my heart,
How could I bear to hear thy voice
  Pronounce the word,—Depart!

3 O! wretched state of deep despair,
  To see my God remove,
And fix my doleful station where
  I must not taste his love.

AWAKENING.

DUNDEE. C. M.

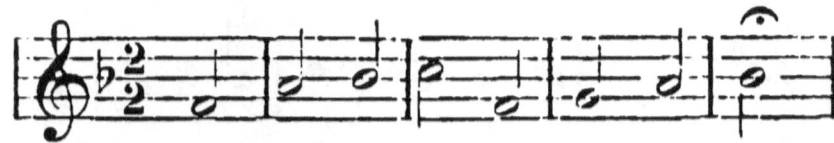

44

SINNERS, the voice of God regard;
  'Tis mercy speaks to-day;
He calls you by his sacred word
  From sin's destructive way.

2 Your way is dark, and leads to hell;
  Why will you persevere?
Can you in endless torments dwell,
  Shut up in black despair?

3 Why will you in the crooked ways
  Of sin and folly go?
In pain you travel all your days,
  To reach eternal wo.

4 But he that turns to God shall live,
  Through his abounding grace;
His mercy will the guilt forgive
  Of those that seek his face.
                                   FAWCETT.

45

BENEATH our feet and o'er our head,
  Is equal warning given;
Beneath us lie the countless dead,—
  Above us is the heaven.

2 Death rides on every passing breeze,
  And lurks in every flower;
Each season has its own disease,—
  Its peril every hour.

3 Turn, mortal, turn; thy danger know:
   Where'er thy foot can tread,
The earth rings hollow from below,
   And warns thee by her dead.

4 Turn, mortal, turn; thy soul apply
   To truths divinely given:
The dead who underneath thee lie,
   Shall live for hell or heaven.

HEBER.

CHINA.   C. M.

46

VAIN man, thy fond pursuits forbear;
   Repent, thine end is nigh;
Death, at the farthest can't be far;
   O think, before thou die.

2 Reflect, thou hast a soul to save;
   Thy sins how high they mount!
What are thy hopes beyond the grave?
   How stands that dark account?

3 Death enters, and there's no defence;
   His time there's none can tell;
He'll in a moment call thee hence,
   To heaven, or down to hell.

4 Thy flesh (perhaps thy greatest care)
   Shall into dust consume;
But, ah! destruction stops not there;
   Sin kills beyond the tomb.

HART.

40 AWAKENING.

BENEVENTO. 7th P. M.

47

SINNERS, turn; why will ye die?
God, your Maker, asks you why—
God, who did your being give,
Made you with himself to live;
He the fatal cause demands;
Asks the work of his own hands,—
Why, ye thankless creatures, why
Will ye cross his love and die?

2 Sinners, turn; why will ye die?
God, your Saviour, asks you why—
He, who did your souls retrieve—
Died himself, that ye might live.
Will ye let him die in vain?
Crucify your Lord again?
Why, ye ransom'd sinners, why
Will ye slight his grace, and die?

3 Sinners, turn; why will ye die?
God, the Spirit, asks you why—
He, who all your lives hath strove—
Urged you to embrace his love.
Will ye not his grace receive?
Will ye still refuse to live?
O ye dying sinners, why,
Why will ye forever die?

C. WESLEY.

AWAKENING.

MARTYN. 7th P. M.

48
SINNERS turn, while God is near;
Dare not think him insincere:
Now, e'en now, your Saviour stands;
All day long he spreads his hands—
Cries,—Ye will not happy be;
No, ye will not come to me,—
Me, who life to none deny:
Why will ye resolve to die?

2 Turn, he cries, ye sinners, turn:
By his life, your God hath sworn,
He would have you turn and live;
He would all the world receive.
If your death were his delight,
Would he you to life invite?
Would he ask, beseech, and cry,—
Why will ye resolve to die?

3 What could your Redeemer do,
More than he hath done for you?
To procure your peace with God,
Could he more than shed his blood?
After all his flow of love,—
All his drawings from above,—
Why will ye your Lord deny?
Why will ye resolve to die?

C. WESLEY.

4*

AWAKENING.

AMSTERDAM.   11th P. M.

49

STOP, poor sinners, stop and think
  Before you further go!
Will you sport upon the brink
  Of everlasting wo?
On the verge of ruin stop;
  Now the friendly warning take;
Stay your footsteps, ere you drop
  Into the burning lake.

2 Say, have you an arm like God,
    That you his will oppose?
  Fear you not that iron rod
    With which he breaks his foes?
  Can you stand in that dread day
    When He judgment shall proclaim,—
  When the earth shall melt away
    Like wax before the flame?

3 Ghastly death will quickly come
    And drag you to his bar;
  Then to hear your awful doom
    Will fill you with despair!
  Sinners then in vain will call—
    Those who now despise his grace—
  "Rocks and mountains on us fall,
    And hide us from his face."

NEWTON.

THE JUDGMENT DAY. C. M.

50

AND must I be to judgment brought,
   And answer in that day
For every vain and idle thought,
   And every word I say?

2 Yes, every secret of my heart
   Shall shortly be made known,
And I receive my just desert
   For all that I have done.

3 How careful then ought I to live—
   With what religious fear—
Who such a strict account must give
   For my behaviour here.

4 Thou awful Judge of quick and dead,
   The watchful power bestow;
So shall I to my ways take heed,—
   To all I speak or do.

5 If now thou standest at the door,
   O let me feel thee near;
And make my peace with God, before
   I at thy bar appear.

CHORUS.

   The Judgment day is rolling round;
   The Judgment day is rolling round;
   The Judgment day is rolling round;
   Prepare to meet thy God.

C. WESLEY.

AWAKENING.

NUREMBURG.   6th P. M.

51

O YE young, ye gay, ye proud;
  You must die and wear the shroud.
Time will rob you of your bloom;
Death will drag you to to the tomb;
    Then you'll cry, and want to be
    Happy in eternity.

2 Will you go to heaven? or hell?
  One you must, and there to dwell:
Christ will come, and quickly too:
I must meet him, and so must you.

3 The white throne will soon appear—
All the world must then draw near;
Sinners will be driven down—
Saints will wear the starry crown.

WILLOUGHBY.   4th P. M.

52

LO! on a narrow neck of land,
  'Twixt two unbounded seas, I stand,
    Secure, insensible:
A point of time, a moment's space,
Removes me to that heavenly place,
    Or shuts me up in hell.

2 O God, mine inmost soul convert,
  And deeply on my thoughtful heart
    Eternal things impress:
  Give me to feel their solemn weight,
  And tremble on the brink of fate,
    And wake to righteousness.

3 Before me place, in dread array,
  The pomp of that tremendous day,
    When thou with clouds shalt come
  To judge the nations at thy bar;
  And tell me, Lord, shall I be there,
    To meet a joyful doom?

C. WESLEY.

TALMAR. 8s & 7s.

53

LISTEN to the gentle promptings
  Of the Spirit's warning voice.
Will ye heed his solemn warnings?
  Can ye slight his wondrous love?

2 Sweetly calling on the erring,
    Pardons offered without price;
  Come, and round the altar kneeling,
    O receive the offered grace.

3 Joy and hope the troubled conscience
    Will allay with soothing peace:
  Press ye then to realms of glory,
    Run with joy the offered race.

46 AWAKENING.

Passing Away.

54

TO-DAY if you will hear his voice,
Now is the time to make your choice:
Say, will you to Mount Zion go?
Say, will you have this Christ, or no?
  We are passing away
   To the great Judgment day.

2 Ye wandering souls, who find no rest,
Say, will you be forever blest?
Will you be saved from sin and Hell?
Will you with Christ in glory dwell?

3 Come now, dear youth, for ruin bound,
Obey the Gospel's joyful sound.
Come, go with us, and you shall prove
The joy of Christ's redeeming love.

4 Leave all your sports and glittering toys·
Come share with us eternal joys.
Or, must we leave you bound to Hell?
Then, dear young friends, a long farewell!

Uxbridge.   L. M.

55

BEHOLD, a stranger at the door;
He gently knocks—has knocked before:

Hath waited long, is waiting still;
You treat no other friend so ill.

2 O lovely attitude! He stands
With melting heart and outstretched hands!
O matchless kindness! And he shows
This matchless kindness to his foes.

3 Admit him ere his anger burn—
His feet depart ne'er to return;
Admit him, or the hour's at hand,
You'll at his door rejected stand.

ZION SONGSTER, 1833.

PHILIPS. C. M.

56
THERE is an hour when I must part
    With all I hold most dear;
And life, with its best hopes, will then
    As nothingness appear.

2 There is an hour when I must stand
    Before the judgment-seat,
And all my sins and all my foes
    In awful vision meet.

3 There is an hour when I must look
    On vast eternity,
And nameless woe or blissful life
    My endless portion be.

4 O Saviour, then, in all my need,
    Be near, be near to me;
And let my soul, by steadfast faith,
    Find life and heaven in thee.

AWAKENING.

HENDON.

57

H ASTEN, sinner, to be wise!
  Stay not for the morrow's sun:
Wisdom, if you still despise,
  Harder is it to be won.

2 Hasten, mercy to implore!
   Stay not for the morrow's sun,
  Lest thy season should be o'er
   Ere this evening's stage be run.

3 Hasten, sinner, to return!
   Stay not for the morrow's sun,
  Lest thy lamp should fail to burn
   Ere salvation's work is done.

4 Hasten, sinner, to be blest!
   Stay not for the morrow's sun,
  Lest perdition thee arrest
   Ere the morrow is begun.
                                    T. SCOTT.

DUNDEE.   C. M.

58

D ARK was the night, and cold the ground
  On which the Lord was laid;
His sweat, like drops of blood, ran down;
  In agony he prayed:

2 "Father, remove this bitter cup,
   If such thy sacred will;
If not, content to drink it up,
   Thy pleasure I fulfill."

3 Go to the garden, sinner; see
   Those precious drops that flow;
The heavy load he bore for thee;
   For thee he lies so low!

4 Then learn of him the cross to bear;
   Thy Father's will obey;
And when temptations press thee near,
   Awake to watch and pray.

59

O SAY not, "I will yet delay
   To seek God's offered grace;"
When Jesus, with a voice of love,
   Says now, "Seek thou my face."

2 Say not, "To-morrow I will turn;"
   To thee it may not come;
For e'en this night thy soul may hear
   Its everlasting doom.

3 Say not, "When sickness lays me low
   I will begin to pray;"
For swift disease or sudden death
   May call thy soul away.

4 But say with earnestness and faith,
   "Jesus, I come to thee;
Now, from this moment, by thy grace,
   Help me from sin to flee."

50   AWAKENING.

EXPOSTULATION.

60

DELAY not, delay not, O sinner, draw near;
  The waters of life are now flowing for thee;
No price is demanded, the Saviour is here,
  Redemption is purchased, salvation is free.

2 Delay not, delay not, why longer abuse
  The love and compassion of Jesus thy God?
A fountain is opened; how canst thou refuse
  To wash and be cleansed in his pardoning blood.

3 Delay not, delay not, O sinner, to come;
  For Mercy still lingers, and calls thee to-day:
Her voice is not heard in the vale of the tomb;
  Her message, unheeded, will soon pass away.

4 Delay not, delay not—the Spirit of grace;
  Long grieved and resisted, may take its sad flight,
And leave thee in darkness to finish thy race—
  To sink in the vale of Eternity's night.

5 Delay not, delay not—the hour is at hand—
  The earth shall dissolve, and the heavens shall fade;
The dead, small and great, in the judgment shall stand;
  What power, then, O sinner, shall lend thee its aid?
ANDERSON.

61

IN life's joyous morning, while hope still is bright,
  And all thy green pathway is beaming with light,
O come to the Saviour, his mercy embrace,
  And sweetly surrender thy heart to his grace.

2 Soon cares and temptations thy steps will attend;
And sorrow's rude tempest may on thee descend;
What arm can sustain thee—what wisdom can guide,
If Christ the Deliv'rer be not at thy side?

3 His love, if thou seek him, will gird thee with power
In manhood's stern conflicts, and trial's dark hour—
With rich consolations thy anguish assuage,
When stung by affliction, or sinking with age.

4 Then fly to his bosom, and in it find rest
From all that can torture thy frail mortal breast;
No storm there can reach thee—no danger assail;
His might is resistless, his truth cannot fail.
BOOTH'S S. S. HYMNS.

62

O TURN ye, O turn ye, for why will you die,
When God in great mercy is coming so nigh?
Since Jesus invites you, the Spirit says, Come,
And angels are waiting to welcome you home.

2 How vain the delusion, that while you delay,
Your hearts may grow better by staying away;
Come wretched, come starving, come just as you be,
While streams of salvation are flowing so free.

3 And now Christ is ready your souls to receive;
O, how can you question? if you will believe—
If sin is your burden, why will you not come?
'Tis you he bids welcome; he bids you come home.

4 Come, give us your hand, and the Saviour your heart,
And trusting in Heaven, we never shall part;
O, how can we leave you? Why will you not come
We'll journey together, and soon be at home.
BOOTH'S S. S. HYMNS.

III.—INVITING TO JESUS.

NETTLETON.

63

COME, ye sinners, poor and needy,
  Weak and wounded, sick and sore;
Jesus ready stands to save you,
  Full of pity, love, and power:
    He is able,
  He is willing: doubt no more.

2 Now, ye needy, come and welcome,
    God's free bounty glorify;
  True belief and true repentance,—
    Every grace that brings you nigh,—
      Without money
    Come to Jesus Christ and buy.

3 Let not conscience make you linger;
    Nor of fitness fondly dream:
  All the fitness he requireth
    Is to feel your need of him:
      This he gives you,—
    'Tis the Spirit's glimm'ring beam.

4 Come, ye weary, heavy-laden,
    Bruised and mangled by the fall;
  If you tarry till you're better,
    You will never come at all;

INVITING TO JESUS. 53

Not the righteous,—
Sinners Jesus came to call.

6 Lo! the' incarnate God, ascending,
Pleads the merit of his blood:
Venture on him,—venture freely;
Let no other trust intrude;
None but Jesus
Can do helpless sinners good. HART.

TURN TO THE LORD.

64

HARK! the Gospel news is sounding;
Christ has suffered on the tree;
Streams of mercy are abounding;
Grace for all is rich and free.

CHORUS.
Turn to the Lord and seek salvation;
Sound the praise of his dear name;
Glory, honour, and salvation!
Christ the Lord has come to reign.

2 Grace is flowing like a river;
Millions there have been supplied;
Still it flows as fresh as ever,
From the Savior's wounded side.

3 Christ alone shall be our portion,
Soon we hope to meet above—
Bathe in the exhaustless ocean
Of the great Redeemer's love.

5*

INVITING TO JESUS.

SILOAM.   C. M.

65

RETURN, O wanderer, return,
  And seek thy Father's face;
Those new desires which in thee burn
  Were kindled by his grace.

2 Return, O wanderer, return;
  He hears thy humble sigh;
He sees thy softened spirit mourn,
  When no one else is nigh.

3 Return, O wanderer, return;
  The Savior bids thee live:
Come to his Cross, and, grateful, learn
  How freely he'll forgive.

4 Return, O wanderer, return,
  And wipe the falling tear;
Thy Father calls— no longer mourn;
  'Tis love invites thee near.

5 Return, O wanderer, return;
  Regain thy long-sought rest;
The Savior's melting mercies yearn
  To clasp thee to his breast.

COLYER.

66

O WHAT amazing words of grace
  Are in the gospel found!
Suited to every sinner's case,
  Who knows the joyful sound.

2 Poor, sinful, thirsty, fainting souls,
    Are freely welcome here;
Salvation, like a river, rolls,
    Abundant, free, and clear.
3 Come, then, with all your wants and
    Your every burden bring: [wounds;
Here love, unchanging love, abounds,—
    A deep, celestial spring.
4 Whoever will—O gracious word!—
    May of this stream partake;
Come, thirsty souls, and bless the Lord,
    And drink, for Jesus' sake.
                          MEDLEY.

67

HAST thou not heard of Gilead's balm—
    The great Physician there,
Who can thine every fear disarm,
    And save thee from despair?
2 Still art thou overwhelm'd with grief,
    And fill'd with sore dismay?
Still looking downward for relief,
    Without one cheering ray?
3 Lift up thy streaming eyes to heaven;
    The great atonement see;
And all thy sins shall be forgiven:—
    Believe, and thou art free.
4 For thee the Saviour suffer'd shame,
    And shed his precious blood:
Believe, believe in Jesus' name,
    And be at peace with God.
                          HASTINGS.

LENOX. 3d P. M.

68

BLOW ye the trumpet, blow
　　The gladly solemn sound;
Let all the nations know,
　　To earth's remotest bound,
The year of jubilee is come;
Return, ye ransom'd sinners, home.

2 Jesus, our great High Priest,
　　Hath full atonement made;
Ye weary spirits, rest;
　　Ye mournful souls, be glad:
The year of jubilee is come;
Return, ye ransom'd sinners, home.

3 Extol the Lamb of God,—
　　The all-atoning Lamb;
Redemption in his blood
　　Throughout the world proclaim:
The year of jubilee is come;
Return, ye ransom'd sinners, home.

4 Ye slaves of sin and hell,
　　Your liberty receive,
And safe in Jesus dwell,
　　And blest in Jesus live:
The year of jubilee is come;
Return, ye ransom'd sinners, home.
　　　　　　　　　　C. WESLEY.

INVITING TO JESUS.

ROYAL PROCLAMATION. (Golden Chain.)

69

HEAR the royal proclamation—
The glad tidings of Salvation,
Published now to every creature—
To the ruined sons of nature:

Jesus reigns! he reigns victorious
Over Heaven and Earth, most glorious,
Jesus reigns. Jesus reigns.
Jesus reigns.

2 See the royal banner flying!
Hear the heralds loudly crying!
"Rebel sinners, royal favor
Now is offered by the Savior."

3 Ho! ye sons of wrath and ruin,
Who have wrought your own undoing,
Here are life and free salvation
Offer'd to the whole creation.

4 Here are wine, and milk, and honey;
Come and purchase without money:—
Mercy, like a flowing fountain,
Streaming from the holy mountain.

5 Shout, ye saints, make joyful mention,
Christ hath purchased our redemption;
Angels shout the pleasing story
Through the brighter world of glory.
ZION SONGSTER, 1833.

INVITING TO JESUS.

ORTONVILLE. C. M.

70

COME humble sinner, in whose breast
  A thousand thoughts revolve;
Come, with your guilt and fear oppress'd,
  And make this last resolve :—

2 I'll go to Jesus, though my sin
    Like mountains round me close;
  I know his courts I'll enter in,
    Whatever may oppose.

3 Prostrate I'll lie before his throne,
    And there my guilt confess;
  I'll tell him I'm a wretch undone,
    Without his sov'reign grace.

4 I can but perish if I go—
    I am resolved to try;
  For if I stay away I know
    I must for ever die.

JONES.

71

HO! all ye hungry, starving souls,
  That feed upon the wind,
And vainly strive with earthly toys
  To fill an empty mind :—

2 Eternal Wisdom hath prepared
    A soul-reviving feast,
  And bids your longing appetites
    The rich provision taste.

3 Ho! ye that pant for living streams,
    And pine away and die;
Here you may quench your raging thirst
    With springs that never dry.

4 Rivers of love and mercy here
    In a rich ocean join;
Salvation in abundance flows,
    Like floods of milk and wine.

                                      WATTS.

BALERMA.   C. M.

72

AMAZING sight! the Savior stands
    And knocks at every door!
Ten thousand blessings in his hands
    To satisfy the poor.

2 "Behold," he saith: "I bleed and die
    To bring you to my rest;
Hear sinners, while I'm passing by,
    And be forever blest."

3 "Will you despise my bleeding love,
    And choose the way to Hell?
Or in the glorious realms above
    With me forever dwell?"

4 "Say will you hear my gracious voice
    And have your sins forgiven?
Or will you make the wretched choice
    That shuts yourselves from Heaven?"

INVITING TO JESUS.

ROCKINGHAM.   C. M.

73

COME, sinners, to the Gospel feast;
Let every soul be Jesus' guest:
Ye need not one be left behind;
For God hath bidden all mankind.

2 Sent by my Lord, on you I call,—
The invitation is to all :—
Come all the world! come sinner, thou!
All things in Christ are ready now.

3 Come, all ye souls by sin oppress'd,—
Ye restless wand'rers after rest;
Ye poor, and maimed, and halt and blind;
In Christ a hearty welcome find.

4 My message as from God receive;
Ye all may come to Christ and live.
O, let his love your heart constrain,
Nor suffer him to die in vain.

5 See him set forth before your eyes—
That precious bleeding sacrifice!
His offer'd benefits embrace,
And freely now be saved by grace.

C. WESLEY.

74

SINNERS, obey the Gospel word;
Haste to the supper of my Lord:
Be wise and know your gracious day;
All things are ready,—come away.

2 Ready the father is to own,
  And kiss his late-returning son;
  Ready your loving Saviour stands,
  And spreads for you his bleeding hands.

3 Ready the Spirit of his love,
  Just now the stony to remove;
  To' apply and witness with the blood,
  And wash and seal the sons of God.

4 The Father, Son, and Holy Ghost,
  Are ready with their shining host;
  All heaven is ready to resound—
  The dead's alive! the lost is found!
                                    C. WESLEY

75

RETURN, O wanderer, return,
  And seek an injured Father's face;
  Those warm desires that in thee burn
  Were kindled by reclaiming grace.

2 Return, O wanderer, return,
  And seek a Father's melting heart;
  His pitying eyes thy grief discern,
  His balm shall heal thy inward smart.

3 Return, O wanderer, return;
  Thy Saviour bids thy spirit live;
  Go to his bleeding feet and learn
  How freely Jesus can forgive.

4 Return, O wanderer, return;
  And wipe away the falling tear;
  'Tis God who says, "No longer mourn;"
  'Tis mercy's voice invites thee near.
                        UNION PR. M. HYMNS, 58

To-day. 6s & 4s.

76

1 TO-DAY! the Saviour calls;
    Ye wand'rers come:
  O, ye benighted souls,
    Why longer roam?

2 To-day! the Saviour calls—
    For refuge fly:
  The storm of vengeance falls;
    And death is nigh.

3 To-day! the Saviour calls—
    O, hear him now:
  Within these sacred walls
    To Jesus bow.

4 The Spirit calls, To-day!
    Yield to his power;
  O, grieve him not away,
    'Tis mercy's hour.
                        UNION P. M. HYMNS.

St. Thomas. S. M.

77

1 THE Spirit in our hearts,
    Is whispering, "Sinners come!"
  The Bride—the Church of Christ, proclaims
    To all his children, "Come."

2 Let him that heareth say
　　To all about him, "Come!"
Let him that thirsts for righteousness,
　　To Christ the Fountain come.

3 Yes, whosoever will,
　　O, let him freely come;
And freely drink the stream of life;
　　'Tis Jesus bids him come.

4 Lo! Jesus, who invites,
　　Declares, "I quickly come."
Lord, even so! I wait the hour,
　　Jesus, my Saviour, come!

78

COME, weary sinners, come,
　　Groaning beneath your load;
The Saviour calls his wand'rers home;
　　Haste to your pard'ning God!

2 Come, all by guilt oppress'd,
　　　Answer the Saviour's call—
O come, and I will give you rest,
　　And I will save you all.

3 Redeemer, full of love,
　　　We would thy word obey,
And all thy faithful mercies prove;
　　　O, take our guilt away.

4 We would on thee rely;—
　　　On thee would cast our care:
Now to thine arms of mercy fly,
　　　And find salvation there.

C. WESLEY.

INVITING TO JESUS.

HEAVENLY FRIEND.

79

THERE'S a Friend above all others;
    O, how he loves!
His is love beyond a brother's;
    O, how he loves!
Earthly friends may fail and leave us;
This day kind, to-morrow grieve us;
But this friend will ne'er deceive us.
    O, how he loves!

2 Blessed Jesus, wouldst thou know him?
    O, how he loves!
Give thyself e'en this day to him;
    O, how he loves!
Is it sin that pains and grieves thee—
Unbelief and trials tease thee?
Jesus can from all release thee;
    O, how he loves!

3 All thy sins shall be forgiven;
    O, how he loves!
Backward all thy foes be driven;
    O, how he loves!
Best of blessings he'll provide thee;
Naught but good shall e'er betide thee;
Safe to glory he will guide thee;
    O, how he loves!

4 Let us still this love be viewing ;
    O, how he loves !
And though faint, keep on pursuing ;
    O, how he loves !
He will strengthen each endeavor ;
And when passed o'er Jordan's river,
This shall be our song forever :
    O, how he loves !

TOPLADY.   6th P. M.

80

WEARY souls, that wander wide
    From the central point of bliss,
Turn to Jesus crucified ;
    Fly to those dear wounds of his :
Sink into the purple flood :
Rise into the life of God.

2 Find in Christ the way of peace—
    Peace unspeakable, unknown ;
By his pain he gives you ease—
    Life by his expiring groan ;
Rise exalted by his fall ;
Find in Christ your all in all.

3 O, believe the record true ;
    God to you his son hath given ;
Ye may now be happy too—
    Find on earth the life of Heaven :—
Live the life of Heaven above,
All the life of glorious love.   C. WESLEY.

INVITING TO JESUS.

FREDERICK. 27th P. M.

81.

O FLY, mourning sinner! saith Jesus to me;
Thy guilt will I pardon—thy soul will I free;
From the chains that have bound thee my grace shall release,
And thy stains will I wash, and thy sorrows shall cease.

2 Though countless thy sins, and though crimson thy guilt,
Yet for crime such as thine was my blood freely spilt;
Come, sinner, and prove me; come mourner and see
The wounds that I bore when I suffered for thee.

3 Then doubt not my power, deny not my will;
Come needy, come helpless; thy soul I will fill
My mercy is boundless: no sinner shall say
That he sued at my feet, but was driven away.

UN. PR M. H. BK

82.

A FOUNTAIN in Jesus, which always runs free,
For washing and cleansing such sinners as we;
Our sins, though like crimson, made white as the wool;
No lack in this fountain; it always is full.

2 All things are now ready, he invites us to come;
The supper is made by the Father and Son;
Rich bounties, rich dainties, here we may receive —
A living forever, if we will believe.

3 The guests which were bidden refused the call,
For they were not ready, nor willing at all,
To be strip'd of their honor, and part with their store,
For a feast that was given and made for the poor.

4 If they are not ready, and wish to delay,
My house shall be filled, the Father doth say:
The highways and hedges, the halt and the blind
Shall come and be welcome; the Supper is Mine.

SAC. MEL. 134.

INVITATION.

33

SINNER go, will you go
  To the highlands of heaven?
Where the storms never blow,
  And the long summer's given;
Where the bright blooming flowers
  Are their odors emitting,
And the leaves of the bowers
  In the breezes are flitting.

2 Where the saints, robed in white—
    Cleansed in life's flowing fountain—
  Shining beauteous and bright,
    Shall inhabit the mountain.
  Where no sin nor dismay,
    Neither trouble nor sorrow,
  Shall be felt for a day,
    Nor be feared for the morrow.

3 He's prepared thee a home;
    Sinner, canst thou believe it?
  And invites thee to come;
    Sinner, will thou receive it?
  O, come, sinner, come,
    For the tide is receding,
  And the Saviour will soon
    And forever cease pleading.

WARE. L. M.

84

HO! every one that thirsts, draw nigh :
'Tis God invites the fallen race;
Mercy and free salvation buy,—
Buy wine, and milk, and gospel grace.

2 Come, to the living waters come!
Sinners obey your Maker's call;
Return, ye weary wand'rers home,
And find his grace is free for all.

3 See from the Rock a fountain rise;
For you in healing streams it rolls;
Money ye need not bring, nor price,
Ye lab'ring, burden'd, sin-sick souls.

4 Nothing ye in exchange shall give;
Leave all you have, and are, behind;
Frankly the gift of God receive;
Pardon and peace in Jesus find.

J. WESLEY.

85

COME O ye sinners to the Lord,
In Christ to paradise restored:
His proferr'd benefits embrace,—
The plenitude of gospel grace:

2 A pardon written with his blood;
The favour and the peace of God;
The seeing eye, the feeling sense,
The mystic joys of penitence:—

3 The guiltless shame, the sweet distress,
The' unutterable tenderness;
The genuine, meek humility;
The wonder, why such love to me:

4 The' o'erwhelming power of saving grace,
The sight that veils the seraph's face;
The speechless awe that dares not move,
And all the silent heaven of love.
C. WESLEY.

HAMBURG.   L. M.

86

JUST as thou art—without one trace
Of love, or joy, or inward grace,
Or meetness for the heavenly place—
O guilty sinner, come, NOW come.

2 Come leave thy burden at the cross;
Count all thy gains but empty dross;
Christ's grace repays all earthly loss;—
O needy sinner come.

3 Come, hither bring thy boding fears,
Thy aching heart, thy bursting tears;
'Tis mercy's voice salutes thine ears;—
O trembling sinner come.

4 The Spirit and the bride say "Come!"
Rejoicing saints re-echo, "Come!" [come;
Who faints, who thirsts, who will, may
Thy Saviour bids thee come.
BOOTH'S S. S. HYMNS.

INVITING TO JESUS.

WILL YOU GO?

87

WE'RE travelling home to Heaven above;
    Will you go? Will you go?
To sing the Saviour's dying love;
    Will you go? Will you go?
Millions have reached that blest abode,
Anointed kings and priests to God,
And millions more are on the road;
    Will you go? Will you go?

2 We're going to walk the plains of light;
    Will you go?
Far, far from death and curse and night;
    Will you go?
The crown of life we then shall wear,
The conqueror's palm we then shall bear,
And all the joys of Heaven we'll share;
    Will you go? Will you go?

3 The way to heaven is straight and plain,
    Will you go?
Repent, believe, be born again;
    Will you go?
The Saviour cries aloud to thee,
"Take up thy cross and follow me,
And thou shalt my salvation see."
    Will you go?

4 O, could I hear some sinner say,
    "I will go,"
O, could I hear him humbly pray,
    "Make me go."
And all his old companions tell,
"I will not go with you to hell,
I long with Jesus Christ to dwell—
    Let me go."

NUREMBURG.   6th P. M.

88

FROM the cross uplifted high,
  Where the Saviour deigns to die,
What melodious sounds we hear
Bursting on the ravished ear:—
Love's redeeming work is done—
Come, and welcome, sinner come.

2 Sprinkled now with blood the throne—
Why beneath thy burden groan?
On his pierced body laid,
Justice owns the ransom paid;
Bow the knee! Embrace the Son!
Come, and welcome, sinner come.

3 Spread for thee the festal board
See with richest bounty stored;
To thy Father's bosom press'd,
Thou shalt be a child confess'd,
Never from his house to roam;
Come, and welcome, sinner come.   HAWEIS.

89

SINNERS, Jesus died for you;
Can you doubt his love so true?
Will you spurn him? O beware,
Lest he leave you in despair.

2 On the cross he bled and died;
Sinner see the crucified!
Can you turn from love like this,
When he offers life and peace?

3 In the grave for you he laid,
Wresting terrors from its bed;
Then arose ascending high,
Will you join him in the sky?

4 Come with us to mansions there,
Give up sin, a crown to wear;
Leave this world, a throne to gain;
Fly to Christ and with him reign.

5 In his love we'll ever share;
Joy and peace will gather there;
When we pass the chilling flood,
Then we'll live and reign with God.

SAC. MEL. 121.

90

HARK! my soul, it is the Lord!
'Tis thy Saviour, hear his word;
Jesus speaks, he speaks to thee;
" Say, poor sinner, lov'st thou me?"

2 "Mine is an unchanging love,
   Higher than the heights above—
   Deeper than the depths beneath—
   Free and faithful, strong as death!

3 "Thou shalt see my glory soon,
   When the work of faith is done—
   Partner of my throne shalt be:
   Say, poor sinner, lov'st thou me?"

4 Lord! it is my chief complaint,
   That my love is still so faint;
   Yet I love thee and adore:
   O for grace to love thee more!

   COWPER.

PORTUGUESE HYMN.

91

O THERE is a fountain that never is dry
  The wounds of Immanuel that fountain supply:
From ages to ages the crimson stream flows,
To cleanse the polluted and lighten their woes.

2 No vileness too vile for that fount to remove;
  No sinner too sinful its virtues to prove;
  If conscience reproaches, if terror appal,
  'Twas opened for you, for 'twas opened for all.

3 Then come to the fountain so gushing and red;
  A tempest of wrath mutters over your head,
  And the moments of mercy are passing away.
  Then come to the fountain, poor sinner, to-day.

DENNIS. S. M.

92

Ye wretched starving poor,
　Behold a royal feast!
Where mercy spreads her bounteous store
　For every humble guest.

2 See Christ with open arms
　　Invites and bids you come:
O, stay not back, though fear alarms;
　For yet there still is room.

3 O come, and with us taste
　　The blessings of his love;
While hope expects the sweet repast,
　Of nobler joys above.

4 There, with united voice,
　　Before the eternal throne,
Ten thousand thousand souls rejoice,
　In ecstacies unknown.

5 Ten thousand thousand more
　　Are welcome still to come;
Ye longing souls, the grace adore;
　Approach—there yet is room.
STEELE.

93

Now is the' accepted time;
　Now is the day of grace;
Now, sinners, come without delay,
　And seek the Saviour's face.

INVITING TO JESUS.

2 Now is the' accepted time:
   The Saviour calls to-day;
   To-morrow it may be too late—
   Then why should you delay?

3 Now is the' accepted time,
   The Gospel bids you come;
   And every promise in his word
   Declares there yet is room.

DORELL.

COME TO JESUS.

94

COME to Jesus, pensive mourner;
   He'll receive you, just now.

2 Fly to Jesus, He will save you,
   He will bless you, just now.

3 He is able, He is willing;
   O believe him just now.

4 He'll forgive you, He'll renew you,
   He will cleanse you, just now.

5 Call upon him; He will hear you;
   Trust him fully, just now.

6 Jesus saves me, now I know it;
   Halleluia, Amen.

IV. PENITENTLY SEEKING GOD.

PETERBORO'. C. M.

95

FATHER, I stretch my hands to thee;
   No other help I know:
If thou withdraw thyself from me,
   Ah! whither shall I go?

2 What did thine only Son endure,
   Before I drew my breath!
What pain, what labour, to secure
   My soul from endless death!

3 O Jesus, could I this believe,
   I now should feel thy power;
And all my wants thou wouldst relieve,
   In this accepted hour.

4 How would my weary soul rejoice,
   Could I but see thy face;
Now let me hear thy quick'ning voice,
   And taste thy pard'ning grace.
C. WESLEY.

96

BECAUSE for me the Saviour prays,
   And pleads his death for me,
God has vouchsafed a longer space,
   And spared the barren tree.

2 Time to repent thou dost bestow;
   Now, Lord, the power impart.
And let mine eyes with tears o'erflow,
   And break my stubborn heart.

3 I now from all my sins would turn,
    To my atoning God;
And look on him I pierced, and mourn,
    And feel the sprinkled blood.

4 Forgiveness on my conscience seal;
    Bestow the promised rest;
With purest love thy servant fill,
    And number with the blest.
C. WESLEY.

MEAR.   C. M.

97

I WOULD be thine: O take my heart
    And fill it with thy love.
Thy sacred image, Lord, impart,
    And seal it from above.

2 I would be thine; but while I strive
    To give myself away,
I feel rebellion still alive,
    And wander while I pray.

3 I would be thine; but, Lord, I feel
    Evil still lurks within;
Do thou thy majesty reveal,
    And overcome my sin.

4 I would be thine; I would embrace
    The Saviour, and adore;
Inspire with faith, infuse thy grace,
    And now my soul restore.
REED'S COLL.

PENITENTLY SEEKING GOD.

FOREST. L. M.

98

GOD of my life, what just return
  Can sinful dust and ashes give?
I only live my sin to mourn:
  To love my God I only live.

2 To thee, benign and saving Power,
  I consecrate my lengthen'd days;
While, mark'd with blessings, every hour
  Shall speak thy co-extended praise.

3 Be all my added life employ'd
  Thine image in my soul to see;
Fill with thyself the mighty void;
  Enlarge my heart to compass thee.

4 Prepare, and then possess my heart;
  O take me, seize me from above;
Thee may I love, for God thou art;
  Thee may I feel; for God is love!
C. WESLEY

99

FATHER, if I may call thee so,
  Regard my fearful heart's desire:
Remove this load of guilt and wo,
  Nor let me in my sins expire.

2 I tremble lest the wrath divine,
  Which bruises now my wretched soul,
Should bruise this wretched soul of mine
  Long as eternal ages roll.

3 I deprecate that death alone—
  That endless banishment from thee!
O save, and give me to thy Son,
  Who suffered, wept, and bled for me.
              C. WESLEY.

WINDHAM.   L. M.

100

O FOR a glance of heavenly day,
  To take this stubborn heart away;
And thaw, with beams of love divine,
This heart, this frozen heart of mine.

2 The rocks can rend; the earth can quake;
  The seas can roar; the mountains shake.
Of feeling, all things show some sign,
But this unfeeling heart of mine.

3 To hear the sorrows thou hast felt,
  O Lord, an adamant would melt:
But I can read each moving line,
And nothing moves this heart of mine.

4 Thy judgments too, which devils fear—
  Amazing thought!—unmoved I hear;
Goodness and wrath in vain combine
To stir this stupid heart of mine.

5 But power divine can do the deed;
  And, Lord, that power I greatly need:
Thy Spirit can from dross refine,
And melt and change this heart of mine.
              HART.

PENITENTLY SEEKING GOD.

GREENWOOD. 7th P.M.

101

JESUS, lover of my soul,
  Let me to thy bosom fly,
While the nearer waters roll,
  While the tempest still is high;
Hide me, O my Saviour, hide,
  Till the storm of life is past;
Safe into the haven guide;
  O receive my soul at last.

2 Other refuge have I none;
  Hangs my helpless soul on thee:
Leave, O leave me not alone;
  Still support and comfort me:
All my trust on thee is stay'd;
  All my help from thee I bring;
Cover my defenceless head
  With the shadow of thy wing.

3 Plenteous grace with thee is found,—
  Grace to cover all my sin:
Let the healing streams abound;
  Make and keep me pure within.
Thou of life the fountain art;
  Freely let me take of thee;
Spring thou up within my heart;
  Rise to all eternity.

C. WESLEY.

PENITENTLY SEEKING GOD.

MOURNING WANDERER.   C. M. D.

102

THOU Lamb of God, for sinner's slain,
  To thee I humbly pray:
O heal me of my grief and pain,
  And take my sins away,
Now from this bondage, Lord, release,
  And give the wanderer rest.
Redeemer, Saviour, seal my peace,
  And take me to my breast.

2 Thou wilt not cast a sinner out,
  Who humbly comes to thee;
My gracious Lord, I cannot doubt
  Thy mercy is for me.
O let me now obtain the grace,
  And find my long-sought rest;
Redeemer, Saviour, seal my peace,
  And take me to thy breast.

3 Mere worldly good I do not want;
  Be that to others given;
While only for thy love I pant—
  My all in earth or heaven:
This is the crown I fain would seize, –
  With which I would be blest:
Redeemer, Saviour, seal my peace,
  And take me to thy breast.

C. WESLEY.

PENITENTLY SEEKING GOD.

WARWICK. C. M.

103

O FOR a closer walk with God,—
  A calm and heavenly frame;
A light to shine upon the road
  That leads me to the Lamb.

2 Where is the blessedness I knew,
    When first I saw the Lord?
  Where is the soul-refreshing view
    Of Jesus and his word?

3 What peaceful hours I once enjoy'd!
    How sweet their mem'ry still!
  But they have left an aching void
    The world can never fill.

4 Return, O holy Dove, return—
    Sweet messenger of rest:
  I hate the sins that made thee mourn,
    And drove thee from my breast.

5 The dearest idol I have known,
    Whate'er that idol be,
  Help me to tear it from thy throne,
    And worship only thee.

COWPER

104

LORD, at thy feet, we sinners lie,
  And knock at mercy's door;
With heavy heart, and downcast eye,
  Thy favor we implore.

2 Without thy grace, we sink oppress'd
   Down to the gates of hell!
 O give our troubled spirits rest,—
   Our gloomy fears dispel.

3 'Tis mercy, MERCY, now we plead;
   Let thy compassions move—
 Mercy that led thee once to bleed,
   In tenderness and love.

4 In mercy now for Jesus' sake,
   O God, our sins forgive;
 Thy grace our stubborn hearts can break,
   And breaking, bid us live.
                                   BROWN.

SHAWMUT.

105
 DID Christ o'er sinners weep,
   And shall our cheeks be dry?
 Let floods of penitential grief,
   Burst forth from every eye.

2 The Son of God in tears
   The wondering angels see;
 Be thou astonished, O my soul!
   He sheds those tears for thee!

3 He wept that we might weep;
   Each sin demands a tear;
 In heaven alone no sin is found,
   And there's no weeping there.
                                   BEDDOME.

PENITENTLY SEEKING GOD.

GANGES.   4th P. M.

106

O THOU who hast our sorrows borne,
  Help us to look on thee and mourn—
    On thee whom we have slain;—
Have pierced a thousand thousand times,
And, by reiterated crimes,
    Renew'd thy sacred pain.

2 O give us eyes of faith to see
The man transfixed on Calvary—
    To know thee, who thou art:
The one eternal God and true!
And let the sight affect, subdue,
    And break my stubborn heart.

3 Lover of souls, to rescue mine,
Reveal the charity divine
    That suffered in my stead:—
That made thy soul a sacrifice,
And quenched in death those flaming eyes,
    And bowed that sacred head.

4 The veil of unbelief remove;
And by thy manifested love,
    And by thy sprinkled blood,
Destroy the love of sin in me,
And get thyself the victory,
    And bring me back to God.

                      C. WESLEY.

PENITENTLY SEEKING GOD.

AMSTERDAM. 11th P. M.

107

FATHER of our dying Lord,
  Remember us for good;
O fulfil his faithful word,
  And hear his speaking blood.
Give us that for which he prays:
  Father, glorify thy Son;
Show his truth, and power, and grace,
  And send the promise down.

2 True and faithful Witness, thou,
  O Christ, the Spirit give;
Hast thou not received him now,
  That we might now receive?
Art thou not the living Head?
  Life to all thy limbs impart;
Shed thy love, thy Spirit shed,
  In every waiting heart.

3 Holy Ghost, the Comforter,
  The gift of Jesus, come;
Glow our hearts to find thee near,
  And swell to make thee room;
Present with us thee we feel;
  Come, O come, and in us be;
With us, in us, live and dwell,
  To all eternity.

C. WESLEY.

PENITENTLY SEEKING GOD.

BOYLSTON.   S. M.

108

AH! whither should I go,
  Burden'd, and sick, and faint?
To whom should I my trouble show,
  And pour out my complaint?

2 My Saviour bids me come;
  Ah! why do I delay?
He calls the weary sinner home,
  And yet from him I stay.

3 What is it keeps me back,
  From which I cannot part,—
Which will not let the Saviour take
  Possession of my heart?

4 Searcher of hearts, in mine
  Thy trying power display;
Into its darkest corners shine,
  And take the veil away.

5 I now believe, in thee,
  Compassion reigns alone;
According to my faith, to me
  O let it, Lord, be done!

6 In me is all the bar,
  Which thou wouldst fain remove:
Remove it, and I shall declare
  That God is only love.

C. WESLEY

PENITENTLY SEEKING GOD. 87

ORON.   6th P. M.

109

BY thy birth, and by thy tears;
By thy human grief and fears;
By thy conflicts in the hour
Of the subtle tempter's power,—
Saviour, look with pitying eye;
Saviour, help me, or I die.

2 By the tenderness that wept
O'er the grave where Laz'rus slept;
By the bitter tears that flow'd
Over Salem's lost abode,—
Saviour, look with pitying eye;
Saviour, help me, or I die.

3 By thy lonely hour of prayer;
By thy fearful conflict there;
By thy cross and dying cries;
By thy one great sacrifice,—
Saviour, look with pitying eye;
Saviour, help me, or I die.

4 By thy triumph o'er the grave;
By thy power the lost to save;
By thy high, majestic throne;
By the empire all thine own,—
Saviour, look with pitying eye;
Saviour, help me, or I die.

GLENELG.

PENITENTLY SEEKING GOD.

MADRID.   9th P. M.

110

TAKE my heart, O Father! take it;
  Make and keep it all thine own;
Let thy Spirit melt and break it;
  Turn to flesh this heart of stone.
Heavenly Father, deign to mould it
  In obedience to thy will;
And, as passing years unfold it,
  Keep it meek and child-like still.

2 Father, make it pure and lowly,
  Peaceful, kind, and far from strife;
Turning from the paths unholy
  Of this vain and sinful life.
May the blood of Jesus heal it,
  And its sins be all forgiven;
Holy Spirit, take and seal it;
  Guide it in the path to Heaven.
                     BOOTH'S S. S. HYMNS.

TALMAR.   9th P. M.

111

FATHER, hear the blood of Jesus,
  Speaking in thine ear above:
From impending wrath release us;
  Manifest thy pard'ning love.

2 O receive us to thy favour,—
  For his only sake receive;
Give us to the bleeding Saviour;
  Let us by his dying live.

3 To thy pard'ning grace receive them,
  Once he pray'd upon the tree;
Still his blood cries out—Forgive them;
  All their sins were laid on me.

4 Still our Advocate in heaven,
  Prays the prayer on earth begun:
Father, show their sins forgiven;
  Father, glorify thy Son!

C. WESLEY

DUKE ST.   L. M.

112

THOUGH I have grieved thy Spirit, Lord,
  Thy help and comfort still afford;
And let a wretch come near thy throne
To plead the merits of thy Son.

2 A broken heart, my God, my King,
Is all the sacrifice I bring;
Thou God of grace, wilt thou despise
A broken heart for sacrifice?

3 My soul lies humbled in the dust,
And owns the dreadful sentence just;
Look down, O Lord, with pitying eye,
And save a soul condemned to die.

WATTS.

PENITENTLY SEEKING GOD.

WINDHAM. L. M.

113

SHOW pity, Lord, O Lord, forgive;
  Let a repenting rebel live.
Are not thy mercies large and free?
May not a sinner trust in thee?

2 My crimes are great, but don't surpass
The power and glory of thy grace;
Great God, thy nature hath no bound,—
So let thy pard'ning love be found.

3 O wash my soul from every sin,
And make my guilty conscience clean
Here on my heart the burden lies,
And past offences pain my eyes.

4 My lips with shame my sins confess,
Against thy law, against thy grace;
Lord, should thy judgments grow severe,
I am condemn'd, but thou art clear.

5 Yet save a trembling sinner, Lord,
Whose hope, still hov'ring round thy word,
Would light on some sweet promise there,—
Some sure support against despair.
                                    WATTS.

114

STAY, thou insulted Spirit, stay,
  Though I have done thee such despite;
Nor cast the sinner quite away,
  Nor take thine everlasting flight.

PENITENTLY SEEKING GOD. 91

2 Though I have steel'd my stubborn heart,
  And shaken off my guilty fears;
And vex'd, and urged thee to depart,
  For many long rebellious years;—
3 Though I have most unworthy been,
  Of all who e'er thy grace received;—
Ten thousand times thy goodness seen,
  Ten thousand times thy goodness griev'd;
4 Yet, O! the chief of sinners spare,
    In honor of my Great High Priest;
  Nor in thy righteous anger swear
    To' exclude me from thy people's rest.
                                C. WESLEY.

GIVE.   C. M.

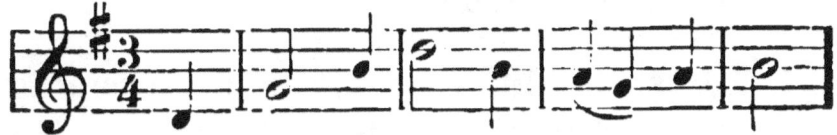

115
O COULD I lose myself in thee—
    The depth of mercy prove,
  Thou vast unfathomable sea
    Of unexhausted love!
2 My humbled soul, when thou art near,
    In dust and ashes lies:
  How shall a sinful worm appear,
    Or meet thy purer eyes?
3 I loathe myself when God I see,
    And into nothing fall;
  Content if thou exalted be,
    And Christ be all in all.
                                C. WESLEY.

PENITENTLY SEEKING GOD.

OLMUTZ. S. M.

116

PROSTRATE at Jesus' feet,
  A guilty rebel lies;
And upward, to the mercy-seat,
  Presumes to lift his eyes.

2 Will justice frown me hence?
  Stay, Lord, the vengeful storm!
Forbid it, that Omnipotence
  Should crush a feeble worm.

3 If sorrows would suffice,
  To pay the debt I owe,   [eyes,
Tears should, from both my weeping
  In ceaseless currents flow.

4 But tears I will not plead,
  To expiate my guilt:—
No tears but those which thou hast shed,
  No blood but thou hast spilt.

5 Think of thy sorrows, Lord!
  And all my sins forgive;
Then justice will approve the word,
  That bids the sinner live.

STENNETT.

117

WHEN shall thy love constrain,
  And force me to thy breast?
When shall my soul return again
  To her eternal rest?

2 Ah! what avail my strife,—
  My wand'ring to and fro?
Thou hast the words of endless life:
  Ah! whither should I go?

3 Thy condescending grace
  To me did freely move;
It calls me still to seek thy face,
  And stoops to ask my love.

4 Lord, at thy feet I fall;
  I groan to be set free;
I fain would now obey the call,
  And give up all for thee.
            C. WESLEY.

PLEYEL'S HYMN.   5th P. M.

118

HOLY Spirit, pity me,
  Pierced with grief for grieving thee;
Present, though I mourn apart,
Listen to a wailing heart.

2 Sins unnumbered I confess,
Of exceeding sinfulness;
Sins against thyself alone—
Only to Omniscience known—

3 Deafness to thy whispered calls;
Rashness 'midst remembered falls;
Transient fears beneath the rod;
Treacherous trifling with my God.
            W. M. BUNTING.

PENITENTLY SEEKING GOD.

RETREAT. L. M.

119

JESUS, the sinner's friend, to thee,
Lost and undone, for aid I flee;
Weary of earth, myself and sin:
Open thy arms, and take me in.

2 Pity and heal my sin-sick soul;
'Tis thou alone canst make me whole;
Dark, till in me thine image shine,
And lost, I am, till thou art mine.

3 At last I own it cannot be
That I should fit myself for thee:
Here, then, to thee I all resign;
Thine is the work, and only thine.

4 What shall I say thy grace to move?
Lord, I am sin—but thou art love;
I give up every plea beside,—
Lord, I am lost—but thou hast died.

C. WESLEY.

120

WHEREWITH, O Lord, shall I draw near,
And bow myself before thy face?
How in thy purer eyes appear?
What shall I bring to gain thy grace?

2 Will gifts delight the Lord Most High?
Will multiplied oblations please?—
Thousands of rams his favor buy,
Or slaughtered hecatombs appease?

Can these avert the wrath of God?
Can these wash out my guilty stain?
Rivers of oil, and seas of blood,
Alas! they all must flow in vain!

4 Guilty I stand before thy face;
On me I feel thy wrath abide;
'Tis just the sentence should take place;
'Tis just—but, oh, thy Son hath died!
C. WESLEY.

WARE.   L. M.

121

LORD, I despair myself to heal;
I see my sin, but cannot feel;
I cannot, till thy Spirit blow,
And bid the' obedient waters flow.

2 'Tis thine a heart of flesh to give;
Thy gifts I only can receive;
Here, then, to thee, I all resign;
To draw, redeem, and seal, are thine.

3 With simple faith on thee, I call,—
My light, my life, my Lord, my all:
I wait the moving of the pool;
I wait the word that speaks me whole.

4 Speak, gracious Lord—my sickness cure;
Make my infected nature pure:
Peace, righteousness, and joy impart,
And pour thyself into my heart!
C. WESLEY.

PENITENTLY SEEKING GOD.

SILOAM. C. M.

122

LORD, I approach thy mercy seat,
  Where thou dost answer prayer;
There humbly fall before thy feet;
  For none can perish there.

2 Bowed down beneath a load of sin
  By Satan sorely press'd—
By wars without and fears within,
  I come to thee for rest.

3 Be thou my shield and hiding-place;
  That, sheltered near thy side,
I may rejoice in Jesus' grace,—
  In Jesus crucified.

4 O wondrous love! to bleed and die—
  To bear the cross and shame,
That, guilty sinners, such as I,
  Might plead thy glorious name.

NEWTON.

123

MY God, my God, to thee I cry;
  Thee only would I know;
Thy purifying blood apply,
  And wash me white as snow.

2 Touch me and make the leper clean;
  Purge my iniquity:
Unless thou wash my soul from sin,
  I have no part in thee.

PENITENTLY SEEKING GOD.

3 But art thou not already mine?
  Answer, if mine thou art;
Whisper within, thou love divine,
  And cheer my drooping heart.

4 Behold, for me the Victim bleeds,—
  His wounds are open wide;
For me the blood of sprinkling pleads,
  And speaks me justified.
                                C. WESLEY.

ST. MARTINS.   C. M.

124

O SUN of righteousness, arise
  With healing in thy wing;
To my diseased, my fainting soul,
  Life and salvation bring.

2 These clouds of pride and sin dispel,
  By thy all-piercing beam:
Lighten mine eyes with faith; my heart
  With holy hope inflame.

3 My mind, by thy all-quick'ning power,
  From low desires set free;
Unite my scatter'd thoughts, and fix
  My love entire on thee.

4 Father, thy long-lost son receive;
  Saviour, thy purchase own;
Blest Comforter, with peace and joy
  Thy new-made creature crown.
                                J. WESLEY.

PENITENTLY SEEKING GOD.

KENTUCKY. S. M.

125

1 O THAT I could repent,
  With all my idols part;
And to thy gracious eye present
  An humble, contrite heart;

2 A heart with grief oppress'd,
  For having grieved my God;
A troubled heart, that cannot rest
  Till sprinkled with thy blood.

3 Jesus, on me bestow
  The penitent desire;
With true sincerity of wo
  My aching breast inspire.

4 With soft'ning pity look,
  And melt my hardness down:
Strike with thy love's resistless stroke,
  And break this heart of stone.
                                C. WESLEY.

126

1 O THAT I could revere
  My much offended God!
O that I could but stand in fear
  Of thy afflicting rod!

2 If mercy cannot draw,
  Thou by thy threat'nings move;
And keep an abject soul in awe,
  That will not yield to love.

PENITENTLY SEEKING GOD. 99

3 Let me with horror fly
  From every sinful snare;
Nor longer, in my Judge's eye,
  My Judge's anger dare.

C. WESLEY

ROCKINGHAM. S. M.

127

JESUS engrave it on my heart,
  That thou the one thing needful art;
I could from all things parted be,
But never, never, Lord from thee.

2 Needful is thy most precious blood;
Needful is thy correcting rod;
Needful is thy indulgent care;
Needful thy all-prevailing prayer;

3 Needful thy presence, dearest Lord,
True peace and comfort to afford;
Needful thy promise to impart,
Fresh life and vigor to my heart.

4 Needful art thou, to be my stay,
Through all life's dark and thorny way;
Nor less in death; Thou'lt needful be,
To bring my spirit home to thee.

5 Then needful still, my God, my King,
Thy name eternally I'll sing;
Glory and praise be ever his;
The "one thing needful," Jesus is.

GRACE. 5th P. M.

128

GRACIOUS Spirit—Love divine!
Let thy light within me shine;
All my guilty fears remove;
Fill me with thy heavenly love.

2 Speak thy pard'ning grace to me;
Set the burden'd sinner free;
Lead me to the Lamb of God;
Wash me in his precious blood.

3 Life and peace to me impart;
Seal salvation on my heart;
Breathe thyself into my breast,—
Earnest of immortal rest.

4 Let me never from thee stray;
Keep me in the narrow way;
Fill my soul with joy divine;
Keep me, Lord, forever thine.

Stocker.

129

SOV'REIGN Ruler, Lord of all,
Prostrate at thy feet I fall;
Hear, O hear, my ardent cry,—
Frown not, lest I faint and die.

2 Justly might thy vengeful dart
Pierce this bleeding, broken heart;—
Justly might thy kindled ire
Send me to eternal fire.

PENITENTLY SEEKING GOD. 101

3 But with thee is mercy found,—
Balm to heal my every wound;
Soothe, O soothe this troubled breast,—
Give the weary wand'rer rest.   RAFFLES.

MERCY.   5th P. M.

130

DEPTH of mercy! can there be
Mercy still reserved for me?
Can my God his wrath forbear?—
Me, the chief of sinners, spare?

2 I have long withstood his grace;
Long provoked him to his face;
Would not hearken to his calls;
Grieved him by a thousand falls.

3 Kindled his relentings are;
Me he now delights to spare;
Cries, How shall I give thee up?—
Lets the lifted thunder drop.

4 There for me the Saviour stands;
Shows his wounds, and spreads his hands;
God is love! I know, I feel;
Jesus weeps, and loves me still.
                                C. WESLEY.

REFRAIN.
God is love, I know, I feel;
Jesus weeps, and loves me still;
Jesus weeps; He weeps and loves me still.

PENITENCE.

131

JESUS, let thy pitying eye
  Call back a wand'ring sheep;
False to thee, like Peter, I
  Would fain like Peter weep.
Let me be by grace restored;
  On me be all long-suff'ring shown;
Turn, and look upon me, Lord,
  And break my heart of stone.

2 Saviour, Prince, enthroned above,
    Repentance to impart,
  Give me, through thy dying love,
    The humble, contrite heart:
  Give what I have long implored,
    A portion of thy grief unknown:
  Turn, and look upon me, Lord,
    And break my heart of stone.

3 For thy own compassion's sake,
    The gracious wonder show;
  Cast my sins behind thy back,
    And wash me white as snow:
  If thy bowels now are stirr'd—
    If now I do myself bemoan,
  Turn, and look upon me, Lord,
    And break my heart of stone.

C. WESLEY.

PENITENTLY SEEKING GOD. 103

AYLESBURY. S. M.

132
1 AND can I yet delay
   My little all to give?—
To tear my soul from earth away
   For Jesus to receive?

2 Nay, but I yield, I yield;
   I can hold out no more:
I sink, by dying love compell'd,
   And own thee conqueror.

3 Though late, I all forsake;
   My friends, my all, resign:
Gracious Redeemer, take, O take,
   And seal me ever thine.

4 Come, and possess me whole,
   Nor hence again remove;
Settle and fix my wav'ring soul
   With all thy weight of love.

5 My one desire be this,—
   Thy only love to know;
To seek and taste no other bliss,—
   No other good below.

6 My life, my portion thou;
   Thou all-sufficient art:
My hope, my heavenly treasure, now
   Enter, and keep my heart.
                      C. WESLEY.

V.—FAITH AND ASSURANCE.

Plymouth Dock.   1st P. M.

133

AND can it be that I should gain
   An int'rest in the Saviour's blood?
Died he for me, who caused his pain?
   For me, who him to death pursued?
Amazing love! how can it be,
That thou, my Lord, shouldst die for me?

2 He left his Father's throne above—
   (So free, so infinite his grace!)—
Emptied himself of all but love,
   And bled for Adam's helpless race;
'Tis mercy all, immense and free,
For, O my God, it found out me!

3 Long my imprison'd spirit lay,
   Fast bound in sin and nature's night:
Thine eye diffused a quick'ning ray;
   I woke; the dungeon flamed with light
My chains fell off, my heart was free,—
I rose, went forth, and follow'd thee.

4 No condemnation now I dread,—
   Jesus, with all in him, is mine;
Alive in him, my living Head,
   And clothed in righteousness divine,
Bold I approach the' eternal throne, [own.
And claim the crown, through Christ my

C. WESLEY.

FAITH AND ASSURANCE. 105

WEBB.   7s & 6s.

134

1 I LAY my SINS on Jesus,
    The spotless Lamb of God;
He bears them all, and frees us,
    From the accursed load.
I bring my GUILT to Jesus,
    To wash my crimson stains
White, in his blood most precious,
    Till not a spot remains.

2 I lay my WANTS on Jesus;
    All fulness dwells in him;
He heals all my diseases,
    He doth my soul redeem.
I lay my GRIEFS on Jesus—
    My BURDENS and my CARES;
He, from them all, releases;
    He all my sorrows shares.

3 I rest my SOUL on Jesus—
    Meek, loving, lowly, mild:
I long to be like Jesus,
    The Father's holy child.
I long to be with Jesus
    Amid the heavenly throng—
To sing with saints His praises—
    To join the angels' song.

                                BONAR.

FAITH AND ASSURANCE.

ARLINGTON. C. M.

135

1 IN hope against all human hope—
  Self-desp'rate, I believe,—
Thy quick'ning word shall raise me up;
  Thou wilt thy Spirit give.

2 The thing surpasses all my thought;
  But faithful is my Lord;
Through unbelief I stagger not,
  For God hath spoke the word.

3 Faith, mighty faith, the promise sees,
  And looks to that alone;
Laughs at impossibilities,
  And cries,—It shall be done!

4 To thee the glory of thy power
  And faithfulness I give;
I shall in Christ, at that glad hour,
  And Christ in me shall live.

C. WESLEY.

136

1 JESUS! Redeemer, Saviour, Lord,
  The weary sinner's friend!
Come to my help, pronounce the word,
  And bid my troubles end.

2 Deliverance to my soul proclaim,
  And life and liberty:
Shed forth the virtue of thy Name
  And JESUS prove to me.

FAITH AND ASSURANCE. 107

3 Faith to be healed thou know'st I have,
  For thou that faith hast given;
Thou canst, thou wilt, the sinner save,
  And make me meet for heaven.

4 Thou canst o'ercome this heart of mine;
  Thou wilt victorious prove:
For everlasting strength is thine
  And everlasting love.

C. WESLEY.

BALERMA.   C. M.

137

JESUS to thee I now can fly,
  On whom my help is laid;
Oppressed by sins I lift my eye,
  And see the shadows fade.

2 Believing on my Lord, I find
  A sure and constant aid;
On thee alone my constant mind
  Be every moment stayed.

3 Whate'er in me seems wise, or good,
  Or strong, I here disclaim;
I wash my garments in the blood
  Of the atoning Lamb.

4 Jesus, my strength, my life, my rest,
  On thee will I depend,
'Till summon'd to the marriage-feast,
  When faith in sight shall end.

C. WESLEY.

FAITH AND ASSURANCE.

WARD. L. M.

138
GREAT God, indulge my humble claim;
  Be thou my hope, my joy, my rest;
The glories that compose thy name
  Stand all engaged to make me blest.

2 Thou great and good, thou just and wise,
  Thou art my Father and my God;
And I am thine by sacred ties,—
  Thy son, thy servant bought with blood.

3 With heart and eyes, and lifted hands,
  For thee I long, to thee I look;
As travellers in thirsty lands
  Pant for the cooling water-brook.

4 I'll lift my hands, I'll raise my voice,
  While I have breath to pray or praise;
This work shall make my heart rejoice,
  And fill the remnant of my days.
WATTS.

139
BY faith I to the fountain fly,
  Open'd for all mankind and me,
To purge my sins of deepest dye,—
  My life and heart's impurity.

2 From Christ, the smitten Rock, it flows,—
  The purple and the crystal stream;
Pardon and holiness bestows;
  And both I gain through faith in him.
C. WESLEY.

FAITH AND ASSURANCE.

TOPLADY.   6th P. M.

140

A BBA, Father, hear thy child,
Late in Jesus reconciled;
Hear, and all the graces shower,—
All the joy, and peace, and power;
All my Saviour asks above,
All the life and heaven of love.

2 Lord, I will not let thee go
Till the blessing thou bestow:
Hear my Advocate divine:
Lo! to his my suit I join:
Join'd to his, it cannot fail;
Bless me; for I will prevail.

3 Heavenly Father, life divine,
Change my nature into thine;
Move, and spread throughout my soul;
Actuate, and fill the whole:
Be it I no longer now
Living in the flesh, but thou.

4 Holy Ghost, no more delay;
Come, and in thy temple stay:
Now thine inward witness bear,
Strong, and permanent, and clear:
Spring of life, thyself impart;
Rise eternal in my heart.

C. WESLEY.

STREAMING MERCY.

141

DROOPING souls, no longer grieve;
  Heaven is propitious;
If in Christ you now believe,
  You will find him precious.
Jesus now is passing by,
  Calling mourners to him;
He has died, you need not die;
  Now look up and view him.

2 From his hands, his feet, his side,
    Runs a healing fountain;
  See the heart-consoling tide,
    Boundless as the ocean!
  See the living waters move
    For the sick and dying!
  Now resolve to gain his love,
    Or to perish trying.

3 He has pardons, full and free,
    Drooping souls to gladden;
  Jesus calls, "Come unto me,"
    Weary, heavy laden.
  Though your sins like mountains rise,
    Rise, and reach to heaven;
  Soon as you on him rely,
    All shall be forgiven.

4 Streaming mercy, how it flows!
   Now I know, I feel it;
Half has never yet been told;
   Yet I want to tell it.
Jesus' blood has heal'd my wound—
   O, the wondrous story!
I was lost, but now am found;
   Glory! Glory! Glory!

5 If no greater joys are known
   In the upper regions,
I will try to travel on,
   In this pure religion.
Heaven's here, and heaven's there;
   Glory's here and yonder:
Brightest seraphs shout Amen,
   While all the angels wonder.

ZION SONGSTER, 1833

DEVIZES.   C. M.

142

FATHER of Jesus Christ my Lord—
   My Saviour and my Head,
I trust in thee whose powerful word
   Hath raised him from the dead.

2 Thou know'st for my offence he died,
   And rose again for me;
Fully and freely justified,
   That I might live to thee.

C. WESLEY.

FAITH AND ASSURANCE.

Rockport (or Penitence.)

143

GOD of my salvation, hear,
   And help me to believe;
Simply do I now draw near,
   Thy blessing to receive.
Full of guilt, alas! I am,
   But to thy wounds for refuge flee:
Friend of sinners, spotless **Lamb**,
   Thy blood was shed for me.

2 Standing now as newly slain,
   To thee I lift mine eye;
Balm of all my grief and pain,
   Thy blood is always nigh.
Now as yesterday the same
   Thou art, and wilt for ever be;
Friend of sinners, spotless Lamb,
   Thy blood was shed for me.

3 No good word, or work, or thought,
   Bring I to buy thy grace;
Pardon I accept, unbought,—
   Thy proffer I embrace.
Coming as at first I came,
   To take, and not bestow on thee:
Friend of sinners, spotless Lamb,
   Thy blood was shed for me.

C. WESLEY.

CREATION. 1st P. M.

144

NOW I have found the ground, wherein
Sure my soul's anchor may remain—
The wounds of Jesus, for my sin,
Before the world's foundation slain:
Whose mercy shall unshaken stay,
When Heaven and Earth are fled away.

2 Father, thine everlasting grace
Our scanty thought surpasses far:
Thy heart still melts with tenderness;
Thine arms of love still open are,
Returning sinners to receive;—
That mercy they may taste and live.

3 O love! thou bottomless abyss!
My sins are swallowed up in thee:
Covered is my unrighteousness,
Nor spot of guilt remains on me; [skies,
While Jesus' blood through earth and
Mercy, free boundless mercy, cries.

4 By faith I plunge me in this sea;
Here is my hope, my joy, my rest:
Hither, when Hell assails, I flee;
I look into my Saviour's breast:
Away, sad doubt and anxious fear,
Mercy is all that's written there.

J. WESLEY.

145

W ITH joy we meditate the grace
　　Of our high priest above;
His heart is made of tenderness,
　　His mercies melt with love.

2 He'll never quench the smoking flax,
　　But raise it to a flame;
The bruised reed he never breaks,
　　Nor scorns the meanest name.

3 But is it possible that I
　　Should live and sin no more?
Lord, if on thee I dare rely,
　　THE FAITH SHALL BRING THE POWER.

CHORUS.
　　I will believe, I do believe
　　　　That Jesus died for me—
　　That through his blood, his precious blood,
　　　　I shall from sin be free.

146

M ERCY alone can meet my case:
　　For mercy, Lord, I cry:
Jesus, Redeemer, show thy face,
　　In mercy, or I die.

2 Still sure to me thy promise stands,
　　And ever must abide:
Behold it written on thy hands,
　　And graven in thy side!

3 To this, dear Saviour, will I cleave,
    Thy word is all my plea;
That word is truth, and I believe :—
Have mercy Lord, on me.

MONTGOMERY.

SUFFERING SAVIOUR.   C. M.

147

ALAS! and did my Saviour bleed?
    And did my Sov'reign die?
Would he devote that sacred head
For such a worm as I?

2 Was it for crimes that I have done,
    He groan'd upon the tree?
Amazing pity! grace unknown!
And love beyond degree!

3 Well might I hide my blushing face
    While his dear cross appears—
Dissolve my heart in thankfulness,
And melt mine eyes to tears.

4 But drops of grief can ne'er repay
    The debt of love I owe:
Here, Lord, I give myself away,—
'Tis all that I can do.

REFRAIN.
    O the Lamb, the loving Lamb,
        The Lamb on Calvary.
    The Lamb that was slain, but lives again
        To intercede for me.

FAITH AND ASSURANCE.

HAMBURG. L. M.

148

JUST as I am, without one plea,
  But that thy blood was shed for me,
And that thou bid'st me come to thee,
  O, Lamb of God, I come!

2 Just as I am, and waiting not
To rid my soul of one dark blot,
To thee whose blood can cleanse each spot,
  O, Lamb of God, I come!

3 Just as I am, though tossed about,
With many a conflict, many a doubt—
With fears within, and wars without,
  O, Lamb of God, I come.

4 Just as I am, poor, wretched, blind,
Sight, riches, healing of the mind—
Yea, all I need, in thee to find,
  O, Lamb of God I come!

5 Just as I am, thy love unknown
Has broken every barrier down;
Now to be thine, yea, thine alone,
  O, Lamb of God, I come!

CHARLOTTE ELLIOT.

AMERICA.

149

MY faith looks up to thee,
Thou Lamb of Calvary:
Saviour divine,
Now hear me while I pray;
Take all my guilt away:
O let me from this day,
Be wholly thine.

2 May thy rich grace impart
Strength to my fainting heart—
My zeal inspire;
As thou hast died for me,
O may my love to thee
Pure, warm, and changeless be—
A living fire.

3 While life's dark maze I tread,
And griefs around me spread,
Be thou my guide;
Bid darkness turn to day;
Wipe sorrow's tears away;
Nor let me ever stray
From thee aside.

4 When ends life's transient dream—
When death's cold, sullen stream
Shall o'er me roll;
Blest Saviour, then, in love,
Fear and distress remove;
O, bear me safe above;
A ransom'd soul.

R. PALMER.

FAITH AND ASSURANCE.

LENOX. 3d. P. M.

150

1 ARISE, my soul, arise;
　Shake off thy guilty fears.
The bleeding Sacrifice
　In my behalf appears:
Before the throne my Surety stands,
My name is written on his hands.

2 He ever lives above,
　For me to intercede;
His all redeeming love,
　His precious blood, to plead;
His blood atoned for all our race,
And sprinkles now the throne of grace.

3 Five bleeding wounds he bears,
　Received on Calvary;
They pour effectual prayers,
　They strongly plead for me:—
Forgive him, O forgive, they cry,
Nor let that ransom'd sinner die.

4 The Father hears him pray,
　His dear anointed One:
He cannot turn away
　The presence of his Son:
His Spirit answers to the blood,
And tells me I am born of God.

FAITH AND ASSURANCE. 119

5 My God is reconciled;
  His pard'ning voice I hear:
He owns me for his child;
  I can no longer fear;
With confidence I now draw nigh,
And Father, Abba, Father, cry.

C. WESLEY.

TOPLADY.   6th P. M.

151

ROCK of ages, cleft for me,
  Let me hide myself in thee;
Let the water and the blood,
From thy wounded side which flow'd,
Be of sin the double cure,—
Save from wrath and make me pure.

2 Could my tears forever flow,—
  Could my zeal no languor know,—
These for sin could not atone;
Thou must save, and thou alone;
In my hand no price I bring;
Simply to the cross I cling.

3 While I draw this fleeting breath,
  When my eyes shall close in death,
When I rise to worlds unknown,
And behold thee on thy throne,—
Rock of ages, cleft for me,
Let me hide myself in thee.

TOPLADY.

FAITH AND ASSURANCE.

PORTUGAL. L. M.

152

AUTHOR of faith, eternal Word,
  Whose Spirit breathes the active **flame**;
Faith, like its finisher and Lord,
  To-day, as yesterday, the same:—

2 To thee our humble hearts aspire,
  And ask the gift unspeakable;
Increase in us the kindled fire,
  In us the work of faith fulfil.

3 By faith we know thee strong to **save**:
  (Save us, a present Saviour thou:)
Whate'er we hope, by faith we have;
  Future, and past, subsisting now.

4 To him that in thy Name believes,
  Eternal life with thee is given;
Into himself he all receives,—
  Pardon, and holiness, and heaven.

C. WESLEY.

153

I KNOW that my Redeemer lives—
  What joy the blest assurance gives!
He lives, he lives, who once was dead;
He lives my everlasting Head!

2 He lives, to bless me with his love;
He lives, to plead for me above;
He lives my hungry soul to feed;
He lives, to help in time of need.

3 He lives, and grants me daily breath;
  He lives, and I shall conquer death;
  He lives, my mansion to prepare;
  He lives to bring me safely there.

4 He lives, all glory to his name;
  He lives, my Saviour, still the same.
  What joy the blest assurance gives:—
  I know that my Redeemer lives!

MEDLEY.

NORRIS.   L. M.

154

WE have no outward righteousness,
  No merits or good works, to plead;
We only can be saved by grace;
  Thy grace, O Lord, is free indeed.

2 Save us by grace, through faith alone,—
    A faith thou must thyself impart;
  A faith that would by works be shown;
    A faith that purifies the heart;

3 A faith that doth the mountains move;
    A faith that shows our sins forgiven;
  A faith that sweetly works by love,
    And ascertains our claim to heaven.

4 This is the faith we humbly seek—
    The faith in thy all-cleansing blood;
  That faith which doth for sinners speak—
    O let it speak us up to God!

C. WESLEY

On the Cross.

155

BEHOLD! behold! the Lamb of God,
  On the cross, on the cross!
For you he shed his precious blood,
  On the cross, on the cross!
The rocks do rend, the mountains quake,
While Jesus doth atonement make—
While Jesus suffers for our sake,
  On the cross, on the cross.

2 Come, sinners, see him lifted up,
  On the cross, on the cross!
He drinks for you the bitter cup,
  On the cross, on the cross!
To heaven he turns his languid eyes;
"'Tis finish'd!" now the Conqu'ror cries,
Then bows his sacred head and dies,
  On the cross, on the cross!

3 Where'er I go I'll tell the story
  Of the cross, of the cross!
In nothing else my soul shall glory,
  Save the cross, save the cross!
Yes, this my constant theme shall be,
Through time and in eternity,
That Jesus suffer'd death for me,
  On the cross, on the cross!

4 Let every mourner come and cling
　　To the cross, to the cross!
Let every Christian come and sing,
　　Round the cross, round the cross!
Here let the preacher take his stand,
　　And with the Bible in his hand,
Proclaim the triumphs of the Lamb
　　On the cross, on the cross!
BOOTH'S S. S. HYMNS.

ARMENIA.   C. M.

156

ETERNAL Sun of Righteousness,
　　Display thy beams divine,
And cause the glories of thy face
　　Upon my heart to shine.

2 Light, in thy light, O may I see;
　　Thy grace and mercy prove;
Revived, and cheer'd, and blest by thee,
　　The God of pard'ning love.

3 Lift up thy countenance serene,
　　And let thy happy child
Behold, without a cloud between,
　　The Godhead reconciled.

4 That all-comprising peace bestow
　　On me, through grace forgiven;
The joys of holiness below,
　　And then the joys of heaven.
C. WESLEY.

FAITH AND ASSURANCE.

FOREST. L. M.

157

JESUS, the Lamb of God hath bled;
He bore our sins upon the tree;
Beneath our curse, he bowed his head.
" 'Tis finished!" He hath died for me.

2 See, where before the throne he stands,
And pours the all-prevailing prayer;
Points to his side, and lifts his hands,
And shows that I am graven there.

3 He ever lives for me to pray;
He prays that I with him may reign;
Amen, to what my Lord doth say:
Jesus, thou canst not pray in vain.
C. WESLEY.

COME, YE DISCONSOLATE.

158

COME, ye disconsolate, where'er ye languish;
Come to the mercy-seat, fervently kneel;
Here bring your wounded hearts, here tell your anguish;
Earth has no sorrow that Heaven cannot heal.

2 Joy of the desolate, light of the straying;
Hope of the penitent, fadeless and pure,—
Here speaks the Comforter, tenderly saying,—
Earth has no sorrow that Heaven cannot cure.

3 Here see the bread of life; see waters flowing
　Forth from the throne of God, pure from above!
Come to the feast of love; come, ever knowing—
　Earth has no sorrow but Heaven can remove.
MOORE.

THE FOUNTAIN.

159

THERE is a fountain fill'd with blood,
　Drawn from Immanuel's veins;
And sinners, plunged beneath that flood,
　Lose all their guilty stains.

2 The dying thief rejoiced to see
　That fountain in his day;
And there may I, though vile as he,
　Wash all my sins away.

3 Thou dying Lamb! thy precious blood
　Shall never lose its power,
Till all the ransom'd Church of God
　Are saved, to sin no more.

4 E'er since, by faith, I saw the stream
　Thy flowing wounds supply,
Redeeming love has been my theme,
　And shall be, till I die.

5 Then in a nobler, sweeter song,
　I'll sing thy power to save,　　[tongue
When this poor lisping, stamm'ring
　Lies silent in the grave.
COWPER.

On the Cross.

160

BY faith I view my Saviour dying
On the tree, on the tree.
To every nation he is crying,
Look on me! Look on me!
He bids the guilty now draw near,
Repent, believe, dismiss your fear;
Hark! Hark! what precious words I hear!
"Mercy's free! Mercy's free!"

2 Did Christ when I was sin pursuing
Pity me, pity me?
And did he snatch my soul from ruin?
Can it be, can it be?
O yes! he did salvation bring;
He is my Prophet, Priest and King;
And now my happy soul can sing—
Mercy's free. Mercy's free!

3 Jesus, the mighty God, hath spoken;
Peace to me, peace to me;
Now all my chains of sin are broken;
I am free, I am free!
Soon as I in his name believed,
The Holy Spirit I received,
And Christ, from death my soul reprieved,
Mercy's free. Mercy's free!

FAITH AND ASSURANCE. 127

4 Long as I live I'll still be crying,
   Mercy's free, mercy's free!
And this shall be my theme when dying—
   Mercy's free, mercy's free!
And when the vale of death I've passed—
When lodged above the stormy blast,
I'll sing while endless ages last:
   Mercy's free, mercy's free!

Sac. Mel.

Contrast.   10th P. M.

161

A FOUNTAIN of life and of grace
   In Christ our Redeemer, we see:
For us, who his offers embrace,
   For all, it is open and free:
Jehovah, himself, doth invite
   To drink of his pleasures unknown—
The streams of immortal delight,
   That flow from his heavenly throne.

2 As soon as in him we believe,
   By faith of his Spirit we take;
And, freely forgiven, receive
   The mercy for Jesus's sake!
We gain a pure drop of his love;
   The life of eternity know;
Angelical happiness prove,
   And witness a heaven below.

C. Wesley

FAITH AND ASSURANCE.

THATCHER. S. M.

162
GOD'S holy law transgress'd,
  Speaks nothing but despair;
Convinced of guilt, with grief oppress'd,
  We find no comfort there.

2 Not all our groans and tears,
  Nor works which we have done,
Nor vows, nor promises, nor prayers,
  Can e'er for sin atone.

3 Relief alone is found
  In Jesus' precious blood:
'Tis this that heals the mortal wound,
  And reconciles to God.

4 This is salvation's source;
  And all our hopes arise
From Him, who, hanging on the cross,
  A spotless victim dies.
        BEDDOME.

163
WE by his Spirit prove,
  And know the things of God,—
The things which freely of his love
  He hath on us bestow'd.

2 His Spirit, which he gave,
  Now dwells in us, we know;
The witness in ourselves we have,
  And all its fruits we show.

3 Our nature's turn'd, our mind
  Transform'd in all its powers;
And both the witnesses are join'd,—
  Thy Spirit, Lord, with ours.

4 Whate'er our pard'ning Lord
  Commands, we gladly do;
And, guided by his sacred word,
  We all his steps pursue.
                              C. WESLEY.

ST. THOMAS.   S. M.

164.

FATHER, I dare believe
  Thee merciful and true:
Thou wilt my guilty soul forgive,—
  My fallen soul renew.

2 Come, then, for Jesus' sake,
  And bid my heart be clean;
An end of all my troubles make,—
  An end of all my sin.

3 I cannot wash my heart,
  But by believing thee,
And waiting for thy blood to' impart
  The spotless purity.

4 While at thy cross I lie,
  Jesus, the grace bestow;
Now thy all-cleansing blood apply,
  And I am white as snow.
                              C. WESLEY.

FAITH AND ASSURANCE.

WEBB.   7s & 6s.

165

1. I NEED thee, precious Jesus,
   For I am full of sin;
   My soul is dark and guilty,
   My heart is dead within.
   I need the cleansing fountain,
   Where I can always flee;
   The blood of Christ most precious,
   The sinner's perfect plea.

2 I need thee, precious Jesus,
   I need a friend like thee;
   A friend to soothe and sympathize,
   A friend to care for me.
   I need the heart of Jesus
   To feel each anxious care,
   To tell my every want,
   And all my sorrows share.

3 I need thee, precious Jesus,
   And hope to see thee soon,
   Encircled with the rainbow,
   And seated on thy throne.
   There with thy blood-bought children,
   My joy shall ever be,
   To sing thy praises, Jesus,
   To gaze, my Lord, on thee.

JESUS PAID IT ALL.

166

LET the world their virtue boast,—
　Their works of righteousness;
I, a wretch undone and lost,
　Am freely saved by grace;
Other title I disclaim;
　This, only this, my plea :—
I the chief of sinners am,
　But Jesus died for me.

CHORUS.
　　Jesus paid it all—all the debt I owe.

2 Jesus, thou for me hast died,
　And thou in me wilt live;
I shall feel thy death applied;
　I shall thy life receive :
Yet, when melted in the flame
　Of love, this all my plea,—
I the chief of sinners am,
　But Jesus died for me.

3 Glorious Saviour of my soul,
　I lift it up to thee;
Thou hast made the sinner whole,
　Hast set the captive free!
Thou my debt of death hast paid—
　Hast raised me from my fall;
Thou hast full atonement made;
　My Saviour died for all.

FAITH AND ASSURANCE.

NORRIS.

167

MY hope is built on nothing less
  Than Jesus' blood and righteousness.
I dare not trust the sweetest frame,
But wholly lean on Jesus' name.

2 When darkness seems to veil his face
I rest on his unchanging grace;
In every high and stormy gale,
My anchor holds within the vail.

3 His oath, his covenant and blood,
Support me in the whelming flood:
When all around my soul gives way,
He then is all my hope and stay.

CHANGED FROM GOLDEN CENSER, P. 83.

168

JESUS, thy blood and righteousness
  My beauty are, my glorious dress:
'Midst flaming worlds, in these array'd,
With joy shall I lift up my head.

2 Bold shall I stand in thy great day,
For who aught to my charge shall lay?
Fully absolved through these I am,—
From sin and fear, from guilt and shame.

3 Lord, I believe thy precious blood,—
Which, at the mercy-seat of God,
Forever doth for sinners plead,—
For me, e'en for my soul, was shed.

4 Lord, I believe were sinners more
  Than sands upon the ocean shore,
  Thou hast for all a ransom paid,
  For all a full atonement made.

J. WESLEY.

WOODLAND. C. M.

169

O FOR a faith that will not shrink,
  Though press'd by every foe;
That will not tremble on the brink
  Of any earthly wo;—

2 That will not murmur or complain
  Beneath the chast'ning rod;
But, in the hour of grief or pain,
  Will lean upon its God;—

3 A faith that shines more bright and clear
  When tempests rage without;
That when in danger knows no fear,
  In darkness feels no doubt;—

4 A faith that keeps the narrow way
  Till life's last hour is fled,
And with a pure and heavenly ray
  Illumes a dying bed.

5 Lord, give us such a faith as this,
  And then, whate'er may come,
We'll taste, e'en here, the hallow'd bliss
  Of an eternal home.

BATHURST.

FAITH AND ASSURANCE.

SHIRLAND.

170

1 NOT what these hands have done
    Can save this guilty soul;
  Not what this toiling flesh has borne
    Can make my spirit whole.

2 Not what I feel or do
    Can give me peace with God;
  Not all my prayers and sighs and tears
    Can bear my awful load.

3 Thy work alone, O Christ,
    Can ease this weight of sin;
  Thy blood alone, O Lamb of God,
    Can give me peace within.

4 Thy grace alone, O God,
    To me can pardon speak;
  Thy power alone, O Son of God,
    Can this sore bondage break.

5 I bless the Christ of God:
    I rest on love divine:
  And with unfaltering lip and heart
    I call this Saviour mine.

6 I praise the God of Grace;
    I trust his truth and might;
  He calls me his, I call him mine,
    My God, my joy, my light.

BONAR.

VI.—JOY AND PRAISE.

MADRID.   9th P. M.

171
COME, thou fount of every blessing,
  Tune my heart to sing thy grace:
Streams of mercy, never ceasing,
  Call for songs of loudest praise.
Teach me some melodious sonnet,
  Sung by flaming tongues above:
Praise the mount—I'm fix'd upon it—
  Mount of thy redeeming love!

2 Here I'll raise mine Ebenezer;
  Hither by thy help I'm come;
And I hope, by thy good pleasure,
  Safely to arrive at home.
Jesus sought me when a stranger,
  Wand'ring from the fold of God;
He, to rescue me from danger,
  Interposed his precious blood.

3 O! to grace how great a debtor
  Daily I'm constrain'd to be!
Let thy goodness, like a fetter,
  Bind my wand'ring heart to thee:
Prone to wander, Lord, I feel it—
  Prone to leave the God I love;
Here's my heart, O take and seal it;
  Seal it for thy courts above.

ROBINSON.

JOY AND PRAISE.

Loving Kindness.

172

AWAKE my soul in joyful lays,
And sing thy great Redeemer's praise;
He justly claims a song from thee;—
His loving kindness, O how free!

2 He saw me ruined by the fall,
Yet loved me notwithstanding all;
He saved me from my lost estate;—
His loving kindness, O, how great!

3 When trouble, like a gloomy cloud,
Has gathered thick, and thundered loud,
He near my soul has always stood;
His loving kindness, O, how good!

4 Soon shall I pass the gloomy vale,
Soon all my mortal powers shall fail;
O, may my last expiring breath
His loving kindness sing in death.

5 Then let me mount, and soar away
To the bright world of endless day;
And sing, with rapture and surprise,
His loving kindness in the skies.

ZION SONGSTER, 1833.

173

COME, O my soul, in sacred lays,
Attempt thy great Creator's praise:
But O, what tongue can speak his fame?
What mortal verse can reach the theme?

2 Enthroned amid the radiant spheres,
He glory like a garment wears;
To form a robe of light divine,
Ten thousand suns around him shine.

3 In all our Maker's grand designs,
Omnipotence, with wisdom, shines;
His works, through all this wond'rous frame,
Declare the glory of his Name.

4 Raised on devotion's lofty wing,
Do thou, my soul, his glories sing;
And let his praise employ thy tongue,
Till list'ning worlds shall join the song.
BLACKLOCK

WELLS. L. M.

174

COME, let us tune our loftiest song,
And raise to Christ our joyful strain;
Worship and thanks to him belong,
Who reigns, and shall forever reign.

2 Burn every breast with Jesus' love;
Bound every heart with rapturous joy;
And saints on earth, with saints above,
Your voices in his praise employ.

3 Extol the Lamb with loftiest song;
Ascend for him our cheerful strain;
Worship and thanks to him belong,
Who reigns, and shall forever reign.
WATTS.

MISSIONARY HYMN.

175

COME, let us sing of Jesus,
  While hearts and voices blend;
Come, let us sing of Jesus,
  The sinner's only friend.
His holy soul rejoices,
  Amid the choirs above,
To hear our tuneful voices
  Exulting in his love.

2 We love to sing of Jesus,
    Who wept, our path along;
  We love to sing of Jesus,
    The tempted and the strong:
  We love to sing of Jesus,
    Who died our souls to save;
  We love to sing of Jesus,
    Triumphant o'er the grave.

3 Then let us sing of Jesus,
    While yet on earth we stay;
  And hope to sing of Jesus
    Throughout eternal day:
  For, those who here confess him,
    He will in Heaven confess;
  And faithful hearts that bless him,
    He will forever bless.

BETHUNE.

CONCORD. S. M.

176
COME, ye, that love the Lord,
  And let your joys be known;
Join in a song with sweet accord,
  While ye surround his throne.

2 Th' Almighty God is ours—
  Our Father and our Love;
He will send down his heavenly powers,
  To carry us above.

3 There we shall see his face,
  And never, never sin;
There, from the rivers of his grace,
  Drink endless pleasures in.

4 Yea, and before we rise
  To that immortal state,
The thoughts of such amazing bliss
  Should constant joys create.

5 The men of grace have found
  Glory begun below;
Celestial fruit on earthly ground
  From faith and hope may grow.

6 Then let our songs abound,
  And every tear be dry: [ground
We're marching through Immanuel's
  To fairer worlds on high.

WATTS.

JESUS IS MINE.

177

FADE, fade each earthly joy;
   Jesus is mine:
Break every tender tie;
   Jesus is mine;
Dark is the wilderness;
Earth has no resting place;
Jesus alone can bless;
   Jesus is mine.

2 Tempt not my soul away; Jesus is mine;
Here would I ever stay; Jesus is mine.
Perishing things of clay,
Born but for one brief day,
Pass from my heart away; Jesus is mine.

3 Farewell ye dreams of night: Jesus is mine.
Lost in the dawning light; Jesus is mine.
All that my soul hath tried
Left but an aching void;
Jesus hath satisfied; Jesus is mine.

4 Farewell mortality; Jesus is mine:
Welcome Eternity! Jesus is mine.
Welcome O loved and blest!
Welcome sweet scenes of rest!   [mine
Welcome my Savior's breast! Jesus is

H. BONAR.

LONG TIME AGO.

178

JESUS died on Calvary's mountain,
 Long time ago;
And salvation's rolling fountain
 Now freely flows.

2 Once his voice in tones of pity,
 Melted in woe,
As he wept o'er Judah's city,
 Long time ago.

3 Jesus died—yet lives forever,
 No more to die;
Bleeding Jesus, Blessed Saviour,
 Now reigns on high!

4 Now in Heaven he's interceding,
 For dying men;
Soon he'll finish all his pleading,
 And come again.

5 Christians, let your lights be burning,
 In hope of Heaven;
Waiting for our Lord's returning,
 At dawn or even.

6 When he comes, a voice from Heaven
 Shall pierce the tomb:
"Come ye blessed of my Father,
 Children come home."

SAC. MEL.

WARWICK.   C. M.

179

J ESUS, the Name high over all,
   In hell, or earth, or sky;
Angels and men before it fall,
   And devils fear and fly.

2 Jesus, the Name to sinners dear,—
   The Name to sinners given;
It scatters all their guilty fear;
   It turns their hell to heaven.

3 Jesus the pris'ners fetters breaks,
   And bruises Satan's head;
Power into strengthless souls he speaks,
   And life into the dead.

4 O, that the world might taste and see
   The riches of his grace;
The arms of love that compass me,
   Would all mankind embrace.

5 His only righteousness I show,—
   His saving truth proclaim:
'Tis all my business here below,
   To cry,—Behold the Lamb!

6 Happy, if with my latest breath
   I may but gasp his name;
Preach him to all, and cry in death:
   Behold, behold the Lamb.

                                 C. WESLEY.

LISCHER. 3d. P. M.

180

JOIN all the glorious names
  Of wisdom, love, and power,
That ever mortals knew,
  Or angels ever bore:
All are too mean to speak his worth,—
Too mean to set the Saviour forth.

2 Great Prophet of our God,
    Our tongues shall bless thy Name;
  By thee the joyful news
    Of our salvation came,—
  The joyful news of sins forgiven,
  Of hell subdued, and peace with heaven.

3 Jesus, our great High Priest,
    Has shed his blood and died;
  The guilty conscience needs
    No sacrifice beside:
  His precious blood did once atone,
  And now it pleads before the throne.

4 O, thou almighty Lord,
    Our Conqueror and King,
  Thy scepter and thy sword—
    Thy reigning grace we sing:
  Thine is the power; behold we sit
  In willing bonds beneath thy feet.

WATTS.

FOREST.   L. M.

181

FROM all that dwell below the skies,
Let the Creator's praise arise;
Let the Redeemer's name be sung,
Through every land, by every tongue.

2 Eternal are thy mercies, Lord;
Eternal truth attends thy word:
Thy praise shall sound from shore to shore
Till sun shall rise and set no more.

3 Your lofty themes, ye mortals, bring;
In songs of praise divinely sing;
The great salvation loud proclaim,
And shout for joy the Saviour's name.

4 In every land begin the song;
To every land the strains belong;
In cheerful sounds all voices raise,
And fill the world with loudest praise.
WATTS

182

OF Him who did salvation bring,
I could forever think and sing;
Arise, ye needy,—he'll relieve;
Arise, ye guilty,—he'll forgive.

2 Ask but his grace, and lo, 'tis given;
Ask, and he turns your hell to heaven:
Though sin and sorrow wound my soul,
Jesus, thy balm will make it whole.

JOY AND PRAISE. 145

3 To shame our sins he blush'd in blood;
  He closed his eyes to show us God:
  Let all the world fall down and know
  That none but God such love can show.

4 Insatiate to this spring I fly;
  I drink, and yet am ever dry:
  Ah! who against thy charms is proof?
  Ah! who that loves can love enough?
                                    C. WESLEY.

HAPPY Day.   L. M.

183

O HAPPY day that fix'd my choice
   On thee, my Saviour and my God!
 Well may this glowing heart rejoice,
   And tell its raptures all abroad.

2 O happy bond, that seals my vows
    To Him who merits all my love;
  Let cheerful anthems fill his house,
    While to that sacred shrine I move.

3 'Tis done, the great transaction's done;
    I am my Lord's, and he is mine;
  He drew me, and I follow'd on,
    Charm'd to confess the voice divine.

4 Now rest, my long-divided heart;
    Fix'd on this blissful centre, rest;
  Nor ever from thy Lord depart:
    With him of every good possess'd.
                                   DODDRIDGE.

JOY AND PRAISE.

SILVER STREET.

184

ARISE and bless the Lord,
   Ye people of his choice;
Arise and bless the Lord your God,
   With heart, and soul, and voice.

2 Though high above all praise—
   Above all blessing high,
Who would not fear his holy Name,
   And laud, and magnify?

3 O for the living flame,
   From his own altar brought,
To touch our lips, our souls inspire,
   And wing to heaven our thought.

4 God is our strength and song,
   And his salvation ours;
Then be his love in Christ proclaim'd
   With all our ransom'd powers.
                           MONTGOMERY.

185

O BLESS the Lord, my soul;
   His grace to thee proclaim:
And all that is within me join
   To bless his holy Name.

2 The Lord forgives thy sins—
   Prolongs thy feeble breath;
He healeth thy infirmities,
   And ransoms thee from death.

JOY AND PRAISE. 147

3 He clothes thee with his love—
   Upholds thee with his truth;
And, like the eagle, he renews
   The vigor of thy youth.

4 Then bless his holy Name,
   Whose grace hath made thee whole;—
Whose loving kindness crowns thy days:
   O, bless the Lord, my soul.
MONTGOMERY.

WATCHMAN.   S. M.

186

MY God, my life, my love,
   To thee, to thee I call:
I cannot live if thou remove,
   For thou art all in all.

2 Thy shining grace can cheer
   This dungeon where I dwell:
'Tis paradise when thou art here;
   If thou depart, 'tis hell.

3 The smilings of thy face,
   How amiable they are!
'Tis heaven to rest in thine embrace,
   And nowhere else but there.

4 Thou art the sea of love,
   Where all my pleasures roll—
The circle where my passions move,
   And centre of my soul.
WATTS.

BELOVED. 11s & 8s.

187

O THOU, in whose presence my soul takes delight—
    On whom, in affliction, I call;
My comfort by day, and my song in the night,
    My hope, my salvation, my all.

2 Where dost thou at noontide resort with thy sheep,
    To feed in the pasture of love?
For why in the valley of death should I weep,
    Or alone in the wilderness rove?

3 O, why should I wander, an alien from thee,
    Or cry in the desert for bread?
Thy foes will rejoice when my sorrows they see,
    And smile at the tears I have shed.

4 Ye daughters of Zion, declare, have you seen
    The star that on Israel shone?
Say, if in your tents my beloved has been,
    And where, with his flock, he has gone?

5 His voice, as the sound of the dulcimer sweet,
    Is heard through the shadows of death;
The cedars of Lebanon bow at his feet;
    The air is perfumed with his breath.

6 His lips as a fountain of righteousness flow,
    To water the gardens of grace;
From which their salvation the Gentiles shall know,
    And bask in the smiles of his face.

JOY AND PRAISE. 149

7 He looks, and ten thousands of angels rejoice,
  And myriads wait for his word;
He speaks, and eternity, fill'd with his voice,
  Re-echoes the praise of the Lord.
                                    ZION SONGSTER, 1833.

LYONS.   13th P. M.

188

O WHAT shall I do my Saviour to praise,
  So faithful and true, so plenteous in grace;
So strong to deliver, so good to redeem
The weakest believer that hangs upon him.

2 How happy the man whose heart is set free;
  The people that can be joyful in thee;
  Their joy is to walk in the light of thy face,
  And still they are talking of Jesus's grace.

3 For thou art their boast, their glory, and power;
  And I also trust to see the glad hour—
  My soul's new creation, a life from the dead,
  The day of Salvation that lifts up my head.

4 For Jesus, my Lord, is now my defence;
  I trust in his word; none plucks me from thence;
  Since I have found favour, he all things will do;
  My King and my Saviour shall make me anew.

5 Yea, Lord, I shall see the bliss of thine own;
  Thy secret to me shall soon be made known;
  For sorrow and sadness I joy shall receive,
  And share in the gladness of all that believe.
                                    C. WESLEY.

ANTIOCH.   C. M.

189

JOY to the world, the Lord is come!
  Let Earth receive her King;
Let every heart prepare him room,
  And Heaven and Nature sing.

2 Joy to the Earth, the Saviour reigns!
    Let men their songs employ;   [plains
  While fields and floods, rocks, hills and
    Repeat the sounding joy.

190

HARK, the glad sound! the Saviour comes;
  The Saviour, promised long;
Let every heart prepare a throne,
  And every voice a song.

2 He comes, the pris'ner to release,
  In Satan's bondage held;
The gates of brass before him burst—
  The iron fetters yield,

3 He comes, from thickest films of vice
  To clear the mental ray;
And on the eyes oppress'd with night
  To pour celestial day.

4 He comes, the broken heart to bind—
  The wounded soul to cure;
And, with the treasures of his grace,
  To enrich the humble poor.

                              DODDRIDGE.

191

SALVATION! O the joyful sound!
  What pleasure to our ears!
A sov'reign balm for every wound,
  A cordial for our fears.

2 Salvation! let the echo fly
    The spacious earth around,
  While all the armies of the sky
    Conspire to raise the sound.

3 Salvation! O thou bleeding Lamb!
    To thee the praise belongs:
  Salvation shall inspire our hearts,
    And dwell upon our tongues.

                                        WATTS.

192

O 'TIS delight without alloy,
    Jesus, to hear thy name:
  My spirit leaps with inward joy;
    I feel the sacred flame.

2 My passions hold a pleasing reign,
    When love inspires my breast,—
  Love, the divinest of the train,
    The sov'reign of the rest.

3 This is the grace must live and sing,
    When faith and hope shall cease,
  And sound from every joyful string
    Through all the realms of bliss.

                                        WATTS.

ZION. 8th P. M.

193

O THOU God of my salvation—
My Redeemer from all sin;
Moved by thy divine compassion,
Who hast died my heart to win,
I will praise thee:
Where shall I thy praise begin?

2 Though unseen, I love the Saviour;
He hath brought salvation near—
Manifests his pard'ning favor;
And when Jesus doth appear,
Soul and body
Shall his glorious image bear.

3 While the angel choirs are crying,—
Glory to the great I AM,
I with them will still be vying;
Glory! glory to the Lamb!
O how precious
Is the sound of Jesus' name!

4 Angels now are hov'ring round us,
Unperceived amid the throng;
Wond'ring at the love that crown'd us;
Glad to join the holy song:
Hallelujah,
Love and praise to Christ belong!

C. WESLEY.

JOY AND PRAISE.

ARIEL. 4th. P. M.

194

AWAKED by Sinai's awful sound,
My soul in guilt and thrall I found;
  I knew not what to do;
O'erwhelm'd with guilt, with anguish slain:
"The sinner must be born again,
  Or sink in endless wo."

2 Amaz'd I stood, but could not tell
Which way to shun the gates of Hell;
  For death and Hell drew near.
I strove indeed, but strove in vain!
"The sinner must be born again,"
  Still sounded in my ear.

3 Then to the law I trembling fled;
It poured its curses on my head;
  I no relief could find:
This fearful truth I found remain;
"The sinner must be born again,"
  O'erwhelmed my troubled mind.

4 While thus my soul in anguish lay,
Jesus of Nazareth passed that way;
  I felt his pity move.
The sinner by his justice slain,
Now by his grace is born again,
  And sings redeeming love.

HEBER. C. M.

195

JESUS, the Lord of glory died,
  That we might never die;
And now he reigns supreme, to guide
  His people to the sky.

2 Weak though we are, he still is near,
  To lead, console, defend;
In all our sorrow, all our fear,
  Our all-sufficient Friend.

3 From His high throne in bliss, he deigns
  Our every prayer to heed;
Bears with our folly, soothes our pains,
  Supplies our every need.

4 O Jesus, there is none like thee,
  Our Saviour and our Lord;
Through earth and heaven exalted be,
  Beloved, obey'd, adored.

196

HOW sweet the name of Jesus sounds
  In a believer's ear;
It soothes his sorrows, heals his wounds,
  And drives away his fear.

2 It makes the wounded spirit whole,
  And calms the troubled breast;
'Tis manna to the hungry soul,
  And to the weary, rest.

3 Dear Name, the rock on which I build—
   My shield and hiding place;
My never-failing treasure, fill'd
   With boundless stores of grace.

4 Jesus my Shepherd, Saviour, Friend,
   My Prophet, Priest and King;
My Lord, my Life, my Way, my End;
   Accept the praise I bring.

NEWTON.

AZMON. C. M.

197

WITH pitying eyes the Prince of Peace
   Beheld our helpless grief:
He saw, and (O, amazing love!)
   He flew to our relief.

2 Down from the shining seats above,
   With joyful haste he fled;
Enter'd the grave in mortal flesh,
   And dwelt among the dead.

3 O, for this love, let rocks and hills
   Their lasting silence break;
And all harmonious human tongues,
   The Saviour's praises speak.

4 Angels, assist our mighty joys;
   Strike all your harps of gold;
But when you raise your highest notes,
   His love can ne'er be told.

WATTS.

GOLDEN HILL. S. M.

198

WE who in Christ believe
 That he for us hath died—
We all his unknown peace receive
 And feel his blood applied.

2 Exults our rising soul,
 Disburden'd of her load;
And swells unutterably full
 Of glory and of God.

3 His love, surpassing far
 The love of all beneath,
We find within our hearts, and dare
 The pointless darts of death.

4 Stronger than death or Hell
 The sacred power we prove;
And, conqu'rors of the world, we dwell
 In heaven, who dwell in love.

C. WESLEY

199

THE Lord my Shepherd is;
 I shall be well supplied;
Since he is mine, and I am his,
 What can I want beside?

2 He leads me to the place
 Where heavenly pasture grows—
Where living waters gently pass;
 And full salvation flows.

3 While he affords his aid,
   I cannot yield to fear;   [dark shade,
 Though I should walk through death's
   My Shepherd's with me there.

4 The bounties of his love
   Shall crown my following days;
 Nor from his house will I remove,
   Nor cease to speak his praise.

SHIRLAND. S. M.

200

GRACE—'tis a charming sound—
   Harmonious to the ear;
 Heaven with the echo shall resound,
   And all the earth shall hear.

2 Grace first contrived the way
   To save rebellious man;
 And all the steps that grace display,
   Which drew the wondrous plan.

3 Grace led my roving feet
   To tread the heavenly road;
 And new supplies each hour I meet,
   While pressing on to God.

4 Grace all the work shall crown,
   Through everlasting days;
 It lays in heaven the topmost stone,
   And well deserves our praise.

JOY AND PRAISE.

St. Martin's.　　　　　　　　　　C.M.

201

O FOR a thousand tongues to sing,
　My great Redeemer's praise—
The glories of my God and King,
　The triumphs of his grace.

2 My gracious Master, and my God,
　Assist me to proclaim,—
To spread, through all the earth abroad,
　The honors of thy name.

3 Jesus!—the name that charms our fears,
　That bids our sorrows cease;
'Tis music in the sinner's ears;
　'Tis life, and health, and peace.

4 He breaks the power of cancell'd sin;
　He sets the pris'ner free;
His blood can make the foulest clean;
　His blood avail'd for me.
　　　　　　　　　　　　C. WESLEY.

202

COME, let us join our cheerful songs
　With angels round the throne;
Ten thousand thousand are their tongues,
　But all their joys are one.

2 Worthy the Lamb that died, they cry,
　To be exalted thus:
Worthy the Lamb, our hearts reply,
　For he was slain for us.

JOY AND PRAISE.

3 Jesus is worthy to receive
  Honour and power divine;
And blessings more than we can give,
  Be, Lord, for ever thine.

4 The whole creation join in one,
  To bless the sacred Name
Of Him that sits upon the throne,
  And to adore the Lamb.

WATTS.

ARLINGTON.   C. M.

203

MY God, the spring of all my joys;
  The life of my delights;
The glory of my brightest days,
  And comfort of my nights.

2 In darkest shades, if thou appear,
  My dawning is begun;
Thou art my soul's bright morning star,
  And thou my rising sun.

3 The opening heavens around me shine
  With beams of sacred bliss,
If Jesus shows his mercy mine,
  And whispers I am his.

4 My soul would leave this heavy clay
  At that transporting word—
Run up with joy the shining way,
  To see and praise my Lord.

WATTS.

HARWELL. 9th P. M.

204

HAIL, thou once despised Jesus!
  Hail, thou Galilean King!
Thou didst suffer to release us;
  Thou didst free salvation bring.
Hail, thou agonizing Saviour—
  Bearer of our sin and shame!
By thy merits we find favour;
  Life is given through thy name.

2 Paschal Lamb, by God appointed,
  All our sins on thee were laid:
By almighty love anointed,
  Thou hast full atonement made.
All thy people are forgiven,
  Through the virtue of thy blood;
Open'd is the gate of heaven;
  Peace is made 'twixt man and God.

3 Jesus, hail! enthroned in glory,
  There forever to abide;
All the heavenly hosts adore thee,
  Seated at thy Father's side:
There for sinners thou art pleading;
  There thou dost our place prepare,
Ever for us interceding,
  Till in glory we appear.

BAKEWELL.

JOY AND PRAISE.

CARMARTHEN. 3d P. M.

205

REJOICE, the Lord is King:
  Your Lord and King adore;
Mortals give thanks and sing,
  And triumph evermore.
Lift up your hearts, lift up your voice—
  Rejoice, again I say, rejoice.

2 Jesus, the Saviour, reigns—
    The God of truth and love;
  When he had purged our stains,
    He took his seat above.
  Lift up your hearts, lift up your voice—
    Rejoice, again I say, rejoice.

3 His kingdom cannot fail;
    He rules o'er earth and heaven;
  The keys of death and Hell
    Are to our Jesus given.
  Lift up your hearts, lift up your voice—
    Rejoice, again I say, rejoice.

4 Rejoice in glorious hope;
    Jesus, the judge, shall come,
  And take his servants up
    To their eternal home.
  Lift up your hearts, lift up your voice—
    Rejoice, again I say, rejoice.

C. WESLEY

CONFIDENCE. 13th P. M.

206

ALL glory and praise to Jesus our Lord,
So plenteous in grace, so true to his word;
To us he hath given the gift from above,—
The earnest of heaven, the Spirit of love.

2 The truth of our God we boldly assert;
His love shed abroad, and power in our heart,
Ye all may inherit, on Jesus who call
The gift of his Spirit is proffer'd to all.

3 His witness within, by faith we receive
And, ransom'd from sin, in righteousness live;
Through Jesus's passion we gladly possess
A present salvation,—a kingdom of peace.

4 The peace and the power, ye sinners, embrace,
And look for the shower,—the Spirit of grace;
The gift and the Giver we all may receive.
Forever and ever within us to live.

C. WESLEY.

207

ALL praise to the Lamb! accepted I am,
Through faith in the Saviour's adorable Name:
In him I confide, his blood is applied;
For me he hath suffer'd, for me he hath died.

2 Not a doubt doth arise, to darken the skies,
Or hide, for a moment, my Lord from my eyes;
In him I am blest, I lean on his breast,
And lo! in his wounds I continue to rest.

C. WESLEY.

CORONATION. C. M.

208

ALL hail the power of Jesus' name!
  Let angels prostrate fall;
Bring forth the royal diadem,
  And crown him Lord of all.

2 Ye chosen seed of Israel's race—
  Ye ransomed from the fall;
Hail Him who saves you by his grace.
  And crown him Lord of all.

3 Hail Him, ye heirs of David's line,
  Whom David Lord did call;
The God incarnate, man divine;
  And crown him Lord of all.

4 Sinners, whose love can ne'er forget
  The wormwood and the gall;
Go, spread your trophies at his feet,
  And crown him Lord of all.

5 Let every kindred, every tribe,
  On this terrestrial ball,
To him all majesty ascribe,
  And crown him Lord of all.

6 O that, with yonder sacred throng,
  We at his feet may fall;
We'll join the everlasting song,
  And crown him Lord of all.

PERONNET.

JOY AND PRAISE.

AVON. C. M.

209

1 JESUS, I love thy charming name;
   'Tis music to mine ear:
Fain would I sound it out so loud,
   That earth and heaven should hear.

2 Yes, thou art precious to my soul;
   My transport and my trust;
Jewels, to thee, are gaudy toys,
   And gold is sordid dust.

3 All my capacious powers can wish,
   In thee doth richly meet;
Nor to mine eye is light so dear,
   Nor friendship half so sweet.

4 Thy grace still dwells upon my heart,
   And sheds its fragrance there;
The noblest balm of all its wounds—
   The cordial of its care.

5 I'll speak the honors of thy name
   With my last laboring breath;
Then, speechless, clasp thee in mine arms,
   The antidote of death.

DODDRIDGE.

JOY AND PRAISE.

FOREST. L. M.

210

HAIL! Sov'reign love, that first began
The scheme to rescue fallen man;
Hail! matchless, free, eternal grace,
That gave my soul a hiding place.

2 Against the God that rules the sky
I fought with hands uplifted high;
Despised the offers of his grace,
Too proud to seek a hiding place.

3 Enwrapt in dark Egyptian night—
More fond of darkness, than of light,
Madly I ran the sinful race,
Secure without a hiding place.

4 But God in mercy gave me light—
Awoke my soul from Nature's night;
I felt the arrows of distress
And found I had no hiding place.

5 The awful Judgment came in view;
To Sinai's fiery mount I flew;
Stern Justice cried with frowning face:
"This mountain is no hiding place!"

6 But lo! a heavenly voice I heard,
And mercy for my soul appeared;
She led me by redeeming grace
To Jesus Christ, my hiding place.

JOY AND PRAISE.

THE LORD MY SHEPHERD.

211

THE Lord is my Shepherd, how happy am I;
   He's tender and watchful my wants to supply!
He daily provides me with raiment and food;
Whate'er he denies me, is meant for my good.

2 The Lord is my Shepherd, then I must obey
His gracious commandments, and walk in his way.
His fear he will teach me, my heart he'll renew;
And though I'm so sinful, my sins he'll subdue.

3 The Lord is my Shepherd, how happy am I!
I'm blest while I live, and I'm blest when I die;
In death's gloomy valley no evil I'll dread;
"For I will be with thee," my Shepherd has said.

4 The Lord is my Shepherd, I'll sing with delight,
Till call'd to adore him in regions of light;
Then praise him with angels, with bright harps of gold,
And ever and ever his glory behold.

REV. & CAMP M. MELODIES.

212

O WHO'S like my Saviour; he's Salem's bright king;
   He smiles, and he loves me, and learns me to sing.
I'll praise him, I'll praise him, with notes loud and shrill,
While rivers of pleasure my spirit doth fill.

2 O, Jesus, my Saviour, I know thou art mine;
For thee all the pleasures of earth I resign.
Of objects most pleasing I love thee the best;
Without thee I'm wretched, but with thee I'm blest.

3 Thou art my rich treasure, my joy and my love;
(None richer possessed by the angels above.)
For thee all the pleasure of sense I forego,
And wander a pilgrim despised below.

4 In vain I attempt to describe what I feel;
The language of mortals for ever must fail;
My Jesus is precious—my soul's in a flame;
I'm raised into raptures, while praising his name.

5 I find him in singing, I find him prayer;
In sweet meditation he always is near;
My constant companion, O may we not part!
All glory to Jesus, who dwells in my heart.
Zion Songster, 1833.

213

My soul's full of glory, inspiring my tongue;
Could I meet with angels, I'd sing them a song:
I'd sing of my Jesus, and tell of his charms,
And beg them to bear me to his loving arms.

2 O Jesus! Blest Saviour! thou balm of my soul,
'Twas thou, my Redeemer, that made my heart whole;
O bring me to view thee, thou glorious King—
In regions of glory thy praises to sing.

3 O Heaven! Sweet Heaven! I long to be gone,
To meet all my brethren before the white throne.
Come angels! Come angels! I'm ready to fly!
Come, quickly convey me to God in the sky.

4 A glimpse of bright glory surprises my soul;
I sink in bright visions, to view the bright goal;
My soul, while I'm singing, is leaping to go;
This moment for Heaven, I'd leave all below.
Zion Songster, 1833

WEBB. 26th P. M.

214
HAIL, to the Lord's anointed,
  Great David's greater Son!
Hail, in the time appointed,
  His reign on earth begun!
He comes to break oppression—
  To set the captive free;
To take away transgression,
  And rule in equity.

2 He comes, with succor speedy
  To those who suffer wrong;
To help the poor and needy,
  And bid the weak be strong;
To give them songs for sighing—
  Their darkness turn to light—
Whose souls, condemn'd and dying,
  Were precious in his sight.
MONTGOMERY.

DEVIZES. C. M.

215
BLEST be our everlasting Lord,
  Our Father, God, and King!
Thy sov'reign goodness we record—
  Thy glorious power we sing.

2 By thee the victory is given:
  The majesty divine,
Wisdom and might, and earth and heaven,
  And all therein, are thine.

3 The kingdom, Lord, is thine alone,
  Who dost thy right maintain,
And high on thy eternal throne,
  O'er men and angels reign.

4 Thou hast on us the grace bestow'd,
  Thy greatness to proclaim;
And therefore now we thank our God,
  And praise thy glorious name.
                                C. WESLEY

216

TO Jesus' Name give thanks and sing,
  Whose mercies never end:
Rejoice! Rejoice! the Lord is King;
  The King is now our Friend.

2 We for his sake count all things loss;
  On earthly good look down;
And joyfully sustain the cross,
  Till we receive the crown.

3 Let all who for the promise wait,
  The Holy Ghost receive;
And, raised to our unsinning state,
  With God in Eden live—

4 Live, till the Lord in glory come,
  And wait his heaven to share:
He now is fitting up your home;
  Go on, we'll meet you there.
                                C. WESLEY.

JOY AND PRAISE.

THE LORD IS MERCIFUL.

217

LORD, with glowing heart I'd praise thee,
  For the bliss thy love bestows;
For the pardoning grace that saves me,
  And the peace that from it flows:
The Lord is merciful; the Lord is pitiful;
O, how merciful the Lord has been to me!

2 Help, O God, my weak endeavor;
  This dull soul to rapture raise:
Thou must light the flame, or never
  Can my love be warmed to praise.

3 Praise, my soul, the God that bought thee,
  Wretched wanderer, far astray;
Found thee lost, and kindly brought thee,
  From the paths of death away.

4 Praise, with love's devoutest feeling,
  Him who saw thy guilt-born fear,
And, the light of hope revealing,
  Bade the blood-stained cross appear.

5 Lord, this bosom's ardent feeling
  Vainly would my lips express:
Low before thy footstool kneeling,
  Deign thy suppliant's prayer to bless.

6 Let thy grace, my soul's chief treasure,
  Love's pure flame within me raise;
And, since words can never measure,
  Let my LIFE show forth thy praise.

THE GREAT PHYSICIAN.

218

HOW lost was my condition,
  Till Jesus made me whole;
There is but one Physician
  Can cure the sin-sick soul.
Next door to death he found me,
  And snatched me from the grave,
To tell to all around me,
  His wondrous power to save.

2 The worst of all diseases
    Is light compared to sin;
  On every part it seizes,
    But rages most within:
  'Tis palsy, plague and fever,
    And madness, all combined;
  And none but a believer,
    The least relief can find.

3 A dying, risen Jesus,
    Seen by an eye of faith,
  At once from danger frees us,
    And saves the soul from death.
  Come, then, to this Physician;
    His help he'll freely give;
  He makes no hard condition;
    'Tis only "Look and live."

ZION SONGSTER, 1833.

JOY AND PRAISE.

PLYMOUTH DOCK.   1st P. M.

219

I'LL praise my Maker while I've breath,
  And, when my voice is lost in death,
    Praise shall employ my nobler powers;
My days of praise shall ne'er be past,
While life, and thought, and being last,
  Or immortality endures.

2 Happy the man whose hopes rely
On Israel's God; he made the sky,
  And earth, and seas, with all their train·
His truth forever stands secure;
He saves the' oppress'd, he feeds the poor,
  And none shall find his promise vain.

3 The Lord pours eyesight on the blind;
The Lord supports the fainting mind:
  He sends the lab'ring conscience peace;
He helps the stranger in distress,
The widow and the fatherless,
  And grants the pris'ner sweet release.

ARIEL,   4th P. M.

220

O COULD I speak the matchless worth,
  O could I sound the glories forth,
Which in my Saviour shine!

I'd soar and touch the heavenly strings,
And vie with Gabriel while he sings,
In notes almost divine.

2 I'd sing the precious blood he spilt—
My ransom from the dreadful guilt
Of sin and wrath divine;
I'd sing his glorious righteousness,
In which all-perfect heavenly dress
My soul shall ever shine.

MEDLEY.

No Sorrow There. S. M.

221

I'M glad salvation's free,
And without price or cost;
For had it been for me to buy,
My soul must have been lost.
I'm glad salvation's free;
I'm glad salvation's free;
Salvation's free, for you and me;
I'm glad salvation's free.

2 Once I was blind and lost—
Of sin and sorrow full;
But now I'm saved through Jesus' blood:
I feel it in my soul.

3 And now I'm on the way
To brighter world's above;
I hope to triumph evermore,
Through the Redeemer's love.

ROWLEY. 15th P. M.

222

O HOW happy are they,
  Who the Saviour obey,
And have laid up their treasure above;
  Tongue can never express
  The sweet comfort and peace
Of a soul in its earliest love.

2 That sweet comfort was mine,
  When the favor divine
I received through the blood of the Lamb;
  When my heart first believed,
  What a joy I received,—
What a heaven in Jesus's name!

3 'Twas a heaven below
  My Redeemer to know,
And the angels could do nothing more
  Than to fall at his feet,
  And the story repeat,
And the Lover of sinners adore.

4 Jesus all the day long
  Was my joy and my song:
O that all his salvation might see;
  He hath loved me, I cried;
  He hath suffer'd and died,
To redeem even rebels like me.

5 O, the rapturous height
  Of that holy delight

Which I felt in the life-giving blood!
 Of my Saviour possess'd,
 I was perfectly blest,
As if fill'd with the fulness of God.

C. WESLEY.

GOD IS LOVE.

223

COME, let us all unite and sing:
 God is love, God is love.
While Heaven and earth their praises bring—
 God is love, God is love.
Let every soul from sin awake,
Their harps now from the willows take,
And sing with me for Jesus sake: God is love.

2 O tell to earth's remotest bound: God is love.
In Christ I have redemption found; God is love.
His blood has washed my sins away;
His Spirit turns my night to day;
And now my soul with joy can say: God is love.

3 How happy is our portion here! God is love.
His promises our spirits cheer; God is love.
He is our sun and shield by day;
By night, he near our tents will stay;
He will be with us all the way: God is love.

4 What, though my heart and flesh shall fail: God is love.
Through Christ I shall o'er death prevail: God is love.
Through Jordan's swell, I will not fear;
My Jesus shall be with me there,
My head above the waves to bear: God is love.

ORIOLA, 117.

HAPPY LAND.

224

I HAVE sought round this verdant earth
   For unfading joy;
I have tried every source of mirth,
   But all, all will cloy.
Lord bestow on me
Grace to set the spirit free;
Thine the praise shall be;
   Mine, mine the joy.

2 I have wandered in mazes dark, Of doubt and distress,
I have had not a kindling spark, My spirit to bless;
   Cheerless unbelief,
   Filled my lab'ring soul with grief;
What shall give relief? What shall give peace?

3 I then turned to thy Gospel, Lord, From folly away;
I then trusted thy holy word, That taught me to pray.
   Here I found release,
   Weary spirit here found rest,
Hope of endless bliss, Eternal day.

2 I will now praise my heavenly King—
   I'll praise and adore—
The heart's richest tribute bring, To thee, God of power.
   And in heaven above,
   Saved by thy redeeming love,
Loud the strains shall move, Forevermore.

SAC. MELODIES.

LENOX.

225

LET earth and heaven agree—
 Angels and men be join'd,
To celebrate with me
 The Saviour of mankind:
To' adore the all-atoning Lamb,
And bless the sound of Jesus' name.

2 Jesus! Transporting sound!
 The joy of earth and heaven;
No other help is found—
 No other name is given,
By which we can salvation have;
But Jesus came the world to save.

3 Jesus! Harmonious name!
 It charms the hosts above;
They evermore proclaim,
 And wonder at, his love:
'Tis all their happiness to gaze,—
'Tis heaven to see our Jesus' face.

4 His name the sinner hears,
 And is from sin set free;
'Tis music in his ears;
 'Tis life and victory;
New songs do now his lips employ,
And dances his glad heart for joy.
C. WESLEY.

PORTUGUESE HYMN.

226

Hosanna to Jesus! I'm filled with his praises;
Come, O my dear brethren, and help me to sing;
No theme is so charming, no love is so warming;
It gives joy and gladness, and comfort within.

2 Hosanna to Jesus, who died to redeem us!
I'll serve him and love him wherever I go;
He's now gone to Heaven, the Spirit he's given
To quicken and comfort his children below.

3 Hosanna forever! His grace like a river
Is rising and spreading all over the land
His love is unbounded, to all it's extended,
And sinners are feeling the heavenly flame.

4 Hosanna to Jesus! My soul feels him precious;
In bright beams of glory, he comes from above.
My heart is now glowing, I feel his love flowing:
Hosanna to Jesus! I'll sing of his love.

REVIVAL AND CAMP MEETING MINSTREL.

227

My God, I am thine; what a comfort divine—
What a blessing, to know that my Jesus is mine!
In the heavenly Lamb, thrice happy I am;
And my heart doth rejoice at the sound of his name.

2 True pleasures abound in the rapturous sound,
And whoever hath found it, hath paradise found;
My Redeemer to know, to feel his blood flow,
This is life everlasting—'tis heaven below.

3 Yet onward I haste to the heavenly feast;
That indeed is the fulness, but this is the taste;
And this I shall prove, till with joy I remove
To the heaven of heavens in Jesus's love.
C. WESLEY.

SILVER STREET.   S. M.

228

AWAKE, and sing the song
  Of Moses and the Lamb;
Wake, every heart and every tongue,
  To praise the Saviour's Name.

2 Sing of his dying love;
    Sing of his rising power;
  Sing how he intercedes above
    For those whose sins he bore.

3 Ye pilgrims, on the road
    To Zion's city, sing;
  Rejoice ye in the Lamb of God,—
    In Christ, the' eternal King.

4 Soon shall we hear him say,—
    Ye blessed children, come;
  Soon will he call us hence away,
    To our eternal home.

5 There shall each raptured tongue
    His endless praise proclaim;
  And sweeter voices tune the song
    Of Moses and the Lamb.
HAMMOND.

VII.—THE CHRISTIAN LIFE.

GREENWOOD. 7th P. M.

229

WHILE we walk with God in light,
  God our hearts doth still unite:
Dearest fellowship we prove—
Fellowship in Jesus' love:
Sweetly each, with each combined—
In the bonds of duty join'd,
Feels the cleansing blood applied—
Daily feels that Christ hath died.

2 Still, O Lord, our faith increase;
Cleanse from all unrighteousness:
Thee the' unholy cannot see;
Make, O make us meet for thee:
Every vile affection kill;
Root out every seed of ill;
Utterly abolish sin;
Write the law of love within.

3 Hence may all our actions flow;
Love the proof that Christ we know;
Mutual love the token be,
Lord, that we belong to thee:
Love, thine image, love impart;
Stamp it now on every heart:
Only love to us be given:
Lord, we ask no other heaven.

C. WESLEY.

THE CHRISTIAN LIFE. 181

BOWER OF PRAYER.

230

THOUGH troubles assail, and dangers affright—
Though friends should all fail, and foes all unite,
Yet one thing secures us, whatever betide,
The promise assures us—The Lord will provide.

2 The birds, without barn or storehouse, are fed;
From them let us learn to trust for our bread;
His saints what is fitting shall ne'er be denied,
So long as 'tis written—The Lord will provide.

3 When Satan appears to stop up our path,
And fills us with fears, we triumph by faith;
He cannot take from us (though oft he has tried,)
The heart-cheering promise—The Lord will provide.

4 He tells us we're weak—our hope is in vain—
The good that we seek, we ne'er shall obtain:
But when such suggestions our graces have tried,
This answers all questions:—The Lord will provide.

5 No strength of our own, nor goodness we claim.
Our trust is all thrown on Jesus's Name;
In this our strong tower for safety we hide;
The Lord is our power—The Lord will provide.

6 When life sinks apace, and death is in view,
The word of his grace shall comfort us through:
Not fearing or doubting, with Christ on our side,
We hope to die shouting—The Lord will provide.

NEWTON.

FOUNTAIN. C. M.

231
HOW sweet and heavenly is the sight,
   When those who love the Lord
In one another's peace delight,
   And so fulfil his word.

2 When each can feel his brother's sigh,
   And with him bear a part;
When sorrows flow from eye to eye,
   And joy from every heart.

3 When free from envy, scorn and pride—
   Our wishes all above—
Each can his brother's failings hide,
   And show a brother's love.

4 When love in one delightful stream
   Through every bosom flows;
Where union sweet, and dear esteem
   In every action glows.

5 Love is the golden chain that binds
   The happy souls above;
And he's an heir of heaven that finds
   His bosom glow with love.
                    ZION SONGSTER 1833.

232
JESUS, united by thy grace,
   And each to each endear'd,
With confidence we seek thy face,
   And know our prayer is heard.

2 Still let us own our common Lord,
    And bear thine easy yoke—
A band of love, a threefold cord,
    Which never can be broke.

3 Make us into one spirit drink;
    Baptize into thy name;
And let us always kindly think,
    And sweetly speak the same.

4 Touch'd by the loadstone of thy love,
    Let all our hearts agree;
And ever toward each other move,
    And ever move toward thee.
                    C. WESLEY.

WARD.   L. M.

233

ARISE, my soul, on wings sublime,
    Above the vanities of time;
Let faith now pierce the veil, and see
The glories of eternity.

2 Born by a new, celestial birth,
Why should I grovel here on earth?
Why grasp at vain and fleeting toys,
So near to heaven's eternal joys.

3 Shall aught beguile me on the road—
The narrow road that leads to God?
Or can I love this earth so well,
As not to long with God to dwell?

PENITENCE. 12th P. M.

234

VAIN, delusive word, adieu,
  With all of creature good:
Only Jesus I pursue,
  Who bought me with his blood:
All thy pleasures I forego;
  I trample on thy wealth and pride;
Only Jesus will I know,
  And Jesus crucified.

2 Other knowledge I disdain;
  'Tis all but vanity:
Christ, the Lamb of God was slain—
  He tasted death for me.
Me to save from endless wo
  The sin-atoning Victim died;
Only Jesus will I know,
  And Jesus crucified.

3 Here will I set up my rest;
  My fluctuating heart
From the haven of his breast
  Shall never more depart:
Whither should a sinner go?
  His wounds for me stand open wide;
Only Jesus will I know,
  And Jesus crucified.

C. WESLEY.

SESSIONS. L. M.

235
FATHER, supply my every need;
 Sustain the life thyself hast given;
O grant the never-failing bread—
 The manna that comes down from heaven.

2 The gracious fruits of righteousness,
 Thy blessings' unexhausted store,
In me abundantly increase,
 Nor ever let me hunger more.

3 Let me no more, in deep complaint,
 My leanness, O my leanness! cry:
Alone consumed with pining want,
 Of all my Father's children I.
C. WESLEY.

236
JESUS, the gift divine I know—
 The gift divine I ask of thee;
The living water now bestow—
 Thy Spirit and thyself, on me.

2 For thou of life the fountain art;
 None else can give or take away;
O may I find it in my heart,
 And with me may it ever stay.

3 Thus may I drink; and thirst no more
 For drops of finite happiness;
Spring up, O well, in heavenly power,
 In streams of pure perennial peace.
C. WESLEY.

OLIVET. L. M.

237

MY hope, my all, my Saviour thou;
To thee, lo, now my soul I bow;
I feel the bliss thy wounds impart—
I find thee, Saviour, in my heart.

2 Be thou my strength—be thou my way;
Protect me through my life's short day;
In all my acts may wisdom guide,
And keep me, Saviour, near thy side.

3 In fierce temptation's darkest hour,
Save me from sin and Satan's power;
Tear every idol from thy throne,
And reign, my Saviour, reign alone.

4 My suff'ring time shall soon be o'er;
Then shall I sigh and weep no more:
My ransom'd soul shall soar away,
And sing thy praise in endless day.

238

JESUS, and shall it ever be,
A mortal man ashamed of thee!
Ashamed of thee, whom angels praise—
Whose glories shine through endless days.

2 Ashamed of Jesus!—That dear Friend
On whom my hopes of heaven depend;
No! When I blush, be this my shame—
That I no more revere his Name.

3 Ashamed of Jesus!—Yes, I may,
    When I've no guilt to wash away;
    No tear to wipe, no good to crave;
    No fears to quell, no soul to save.

4 Till then—nor is my boasting vain—
    Till then, I boast a Saviour slain;
    And O, may this my glory be—
    That Christ is not ashamed of me. GRIGG.

ROCKINGHAM.　　　　　　　　　　　L. M.

239

LORD, how secure and blest are they
    Who feel the joys of pardon'd sin;
Should storms of wrath shake earth and sea,
    Their minds have heaven and peace within.

2 The day glides swiftly o'er their heads,
    Made up of innocence and love;
And soft, and silent as the shades,
    Their nightly minutes gently move.

3 Quick as their thoughts, their joys come on,
    But fly not half so swift away:
Their souls are ever bright as noon,
    And calm as summer evenings be.

4 They scorn to seek earth's golden toys,
    But spend the day, and share the night,
In numb'ring o'er the richer joys
    That heaven prepares for their delight.
                                    WATTS.

THE CHRISTIAN LIFE.

ST. THOMAS. S. M.

240

I LOVE thy kingdom, Lord,—
   The house of thine abode,—
The Church our blest Redeemer saved
   With his own precious blood.

2 I love thy Church, O God!
   Her walls before thee stand,
Dear as the apple of thine eye,
   And graven on thy hand.

3 For her my tears shall fall;
   For her my prayers ascend;
To her my cares and toils be given,
   Till toils and cares shall end.

4 Beyond my highest joy
   I prize her heavenly ways;
Her sweet communion, solemn vows,
   Her hymns of love and praise.

DWIGHT.

241

COMMIT thou all thy griefs
   And ways into his hands,—
To his sure trust and tender care
   Who earth and heaven commands;

2 Who points the clouds their course,
   Whom winds and seas obey;
He shall direct thy wand'ring feet,—
   He shall prepare thy way.

THE CHRISTIAN LIFE.

3 Thou on the Lord rely,
  So, safe, shalt thou go on;
Fix on his work thy steadfast eye,
  So shall thy work be done.

4 No profit canst thou gain
  By self-consuming care;
To him commend thy cause,—his ear
  Attends the softest prayer.

J. WESLEY.

IOWA.   S. M.

242

A CHARGE to keep I have;
  A God to glorify;
A never-dying soul to save,
  And fit it for the sky.

2 To serve the present age;
  My calling to fulfil,—
O may it all my powers engage,
  To do my Master's will.

3 Arm me with jealous care,
  As in thy sight to live;
And O, thy servant, Lord, prepare,
  A strict account to give.

4 Help me to watch and pray,
  And on thyself rely,
Assured, if I my trust betray,
  I shall forever die.

C. WESLEY.

THE CHRISTIAN LIFE.

DUANE STREET.   L. M. D.

243

AWAY, my unbelieving fear!
  Fear shall in me no more have place;
My Saviour doth not yet appear,—
  He hides the brightness of his face:
But shall I therefore let him go,
  And basely to the tempter yield?
No, in the strength of Jesus, no,
  I never will give up my shield.

2 Although the vine its fruit deny—
    Although the olive yield no oil,
  The with'ring fig-tree droop and die,
    The fields elude the tiller's toil—
  The empty stall no herd afford,
    And perish all the bleating race,
  Yet will I triumph in the Lord,—
    The God of my salvation praise.

3 In hope, believing against hope,
    Jesus, my Lord, my God I claim;
  Jesus, my strength, shall lift me up;
    Salvation is in Jesus' name.
  To me he soon shall bring it nigh;
    My soul shall then outstrip the wind;
  On wings of love mount up on high,
    And leave the world and sin behind.

C. WESLEY.

THE CHRISTIAN LIFE.

GREENFIELD. 1st. P. M.

244

STILL nigh me, O my Saviour stand,
  And guard in fierce temptation's hour;
Hide in the hollow of thy hand;
  Show forth in me thy saving power:
Still be thy arms my sure defence,
Nor earth nor hell shall pluck me thence.

2 Since thou hast bid me come to thee,
  (Good as thou art, and strong to save,)
I'll walk o'er life's tempestuous sea,
  Upborne by the unyielding wave;
Dauntless, though rocks of pride be near,
And yawning whirlpools of despair.

3 When darkness intercepts the skies,
  And sorrow's waves around me roll,
And high the storms of troubles rise,
  And half o'erwhelm my sinking soul;
My soul a sudden calm shall feel,
And hear a whisper,—Peace; be still!

4. Though in affliction's furnace tried,
  Unhurt, on snares and death I'll tread;
Though sin assail, and hell, thrown wide,
  Pour all its flames upon my head;
Like Moses' bush, I'll mount the higher,
And flourish, unconsumed, in fire.
C. WESLEY.

THE CHRISTIAN LIFE.

BREMEN.   4th P. M.

245

HELP, Lord, to whom for help I fly,
And still my tempted soul stand by
  Throughout the evil day;
The sacred watchfulness impart,
And keep the issues of my heart,
  And stir me up to pray.

2 My soul with thy whole armour arm;
In each approach of sin, alarm,
  And show the danger near:
Surround, sustain, and strengthen me,
And fill with godly jealousy
  And sanctifying fear.

3 Whene'er my careless hands hang down,
O let me see thy gath'ring frown,
  And feel thy warning eye;
And, starting, cry, from ruin's brink,—
Save, Jesus, or I yield, I sink;
  O save me, or I die.

C. WESLEY

246

BE it my only wisdom here,
To serve the Lord with filial fear—
  With loving gratitude:
Superior sense may I display,
By shunning every evil way,
  And walking in the good.

2 O may I still from sin depart;
 A wise and understanding heart,
  Jesus, to me be given:
 And let me through thy Spirit know
 To glorify my God below,
  And find my way to heaven.
C. WESLEY.

CHRISTIAN PILGRIM.
From Golden Chain, by permission of W. B. BRADBURY.

247
CHRISTIANS, I am on my journey;
  Ere I reach the narrow sea,
 I would tell the wondrous story—
  What the Lord has done for me.

CHORUS.
    Glory! glory! Halleluia!
     Though a stranger here I roam,
    I am on my way to Zion—
     I'm a pilgrim going home.

2 I was lost, but Jesus found me—
   Taught my heart to seek his face;
  From a wild and lonely desert,
   Brought me to his fold of grace.

3 Now my soul with rapture glowing,
   Sings aloud his pardoning love;
  Looks beyond a world of sorrow,
   To the pilgrim's home above.

THE CHRISTIAN LIFE.

WEBB. 26th P. M.

248

GOD is my strong salvation;
  What foe have I to fear?
In darkness and temptation,
  My light, my help, is near:
Though hosts encamp around me,
  Firm in the fight I stand;
What error can confound me,
  With God at my right hand?

2 Place on the Lord reliance;
  My soul, with courage wait;
His truth be thine affiance,
  When faint and desolate;
His might thy heart shall strengthen;
  His love thy joy increase;
Mercy thy days shall lengthen;
  The Lord will give thee peace.
MONTGOMERY.

249

O LAMB of God, still keep me
  Near to thy wounded side;
'Tis only then in safety
  And peace I can abide.
What foes and snares surround me!
  What doubts and fears within!
The grace that sought and found me,
  Alone can keep me clean.

2 'Tis only in thee hiding,
   I feel my life secure—
Only in thee abiding,
   The conflict can endure:
Thine arm the vict'ry gaineth
   O'er every hateful foe;
Thy love my heart sustaineth
   In all its cares and wo.

3 Soon shall my eyes behold thee,
   With rapture, face to face;
One half hath not been told me
   Of all thy power and grace;
Thy beauty, Lord, and glory—
   The wonders of thy love,
Shall be the endless story
   Of all the saints above.   W. B. BRADBURY.

STAND UP FOR JESUS.

250

STAND up for Jesus! All who lead his host,
  Crowned with the splendors of the Holy Ghost!
Shrink from no foe, to no temptation yield;
Urge on the triumphs of this glorious field.

2 Stand up for Jesus! Ye of every name!
All one in prayer, and all with praise aflame!
Forget the sad estrangement of the past,
With one consent, in love and peace at last.

3 Stand up for Jesus! Lo! at God's right hand,
Jesus himself for us delights to stand!
Let saints and sinners wonder at his grace;
Let Jews and Gentiles blend, and all our race,
    Stand up for Jesus! Stand up for Jesus! etc.

BETHANY.

251

NEARER, my God, to thee,
  Nearer to thee!
E'en though it be a cross
  That raiseth me!
Still all my song shall be,
Nearer, my God, to thee,
Nearer, my God, to thee,
  Nearer to thee!

2 Tho', like the wanderer,
   The sun gone down—
Darkness be over me—
   My rest a stone;
Yet in my dreams I'd be,
Nearer, my God, to thee,
   Nearer to thee!

3 There let the way appear
   Steps unto heaven;
All that thou sendest me,
   In mercy given;
Angels to beckon me,
Nearer, my God, to thee,
   Nearer to thee!

4 Then with my waking thoughts,
   Bright with thy praise,
Out of my stony griefs
   Bethel I'll raise;

So by my woes to be
Nearer, my God, to thee,
Nearer to thee!
5 Or, if on joyful wing,
Cleaving the sky,
Sun, moon, and stars forgot,
Upward I fly;
Still all my song shall be,—
Nearer, my God, to thee,
Nearer to thee!

COME MY BRETHREN.

252

COME my brethren, let us try
For a little season,
Every burden to lay by;
Come, and let us reason.
What is this that casts you down?
What is this that grieves you?
Speak and let the worst be known;
Speaking may relieve you.
2 Think on what your Saviour bore
In the gloomy garden,
Sweating blood at every pore
To procure your pardon.
View him nailed to the tree,
Bleeding, groaning, dying!
See! he suffered this for THEE,
Therefore, be believing. ZION SONSTER 1833

THE CHRISTIAN LIFE.
Here is no Rest.

253

HERE o'er the Earth as a stranger I roam,
  Here is no rest,—is no rest;
Here as a pilgrim I wander alone,
  Yet I am blest—I am blest.
For I look forward to that glorious day,
When sin and sorrow will vanish away;
My heart doth leap while I hear Jesus say,
  There, there is rest—there is rest.

2 Here fierce temptations beset me around;
  Here is no rest—is no rest.   [surround;
Here I am grieved while my foes me
  Yet I am blest—I am blest.
Let them revile me and scoff at my name—
Laugh at my weeping—endeavor to shame;
I will go forward, for this is my theme:
  There, there is rest—there is rest.

3 Here are afflictions and trials severe;
  Here is no rest—is no rest: [dear,
Here I must part with the friends I hold
  Yet I am blest, I am blest.
Sweet is the promise I read in his word;
Blessed are they who have died in the Lord;
They have been called to receive their reward:
  There, there is rest—there is rest.

SAC. MEL.

VICTORY.

254

JOYFULLY, joyfully, onward I move,
Bound for the land of bright spirits above;
Angelic choristers sing as I come,
    Joyfully, joyfully, haste to thy home!
    Soon, with my pilgrimage ended below,
    Home to that land of delight will I go;
    Pilgrim and stranger no more shall I roam,
    Joyfully, joyfully resting at home.

2 Friends fondly cherished have passed on before;
Waiting they watch me approaching the shore;
Singing to cheer me through death's chilling gloom—
Joyfully, joyfully, haste to thy home!
    Sounds of sweet melody fall on my ear;
    Harps of the blessed! Your voices I hear;
    Rings with the harmony Heaven's high dome—
    Joyfully, joyfully haste to thy home.

3 Death, with thy weapons of war, lay me low;
Strike, king of terrors! I fear not thy blow;
Jesus hath broken the bars of the tomb!
Joyfully, joyfully, will I go home.
    Bright will the morn of eternity dawn;
    Death shall be banished, his sceptre be gone;
    Joyfully then I shall witness his doom;
    Joyfully joyfully, safely at home.

                              REV. W HUNTER.

THE CHRISTIAN LIFE.

The Cross I'll Cherish.

255

1 O WHO'LL stand up for Jesus,
    The lowly Nazarene,
And raise the blood stained banner,
    Amid the hosts of Sin.

CHORUS.
    The cross for Christ I'll cherish,
    Its crucifixion bear;
    All hail reproach or sorrow,
    If Jesus leads me there.

2 O who will follow Jesus,
    Amid reproach and shame?
Where others shrink or falter,
    Who'll glory in his name?

3 Though foes shall madly gather,
    And devils rage and roar,
Who'll chose the fiery furnace,
    With Jesus evermore?

4 My all to Christ is given,
    My talents, time and voice,
Myself, my reputation;
    The lone way is my choice.

5 O Jesus, Jesus, Jesus,
    My all sufficient Friend,
Come fold me to thy bosom
    Even to the journey's end.

MISSIONARY HYMN. 26th P. M.

256

How much of joy and comfort,
   How much of real cheer,
The dear Lord in his kindness
   Gives to his children here.
So gently doth he lead us—
   So happily we move,
That every day our pathway
   Glows with his tender love.

2 Each hour he draweth nearer,
   And when we need to rest,
He folds his arm about us,
   He lays us on his breast:
He gives us living waters,
   With heavenly manna feeds,
And his exhaustless bounty,
   Supplies our many needs.

3 Sometimes a passing shadow,
   Will flit across the mind,
And dim our hope of Heaven—
   Our pleasing prospect blind:
But then his hand he giveth,
   To lead us safe along:
And in a moment changeth
   The mourning sigh to song.

CHILSON.

THE CHRISTIAN LIFE.

Brattle Street.   C. M. D.

257

I HEARD the voice of Jesus say,
  Come unto me and rest;
Lay down, thou weary one, lay down
  Thy head upon my breast.
I came to Jesus as I was,
  Weary, and worn and sad;
I found in him a resting place,
  And he has made me glad.

2 I heard the voice of Jesus say,
  Behold, I freely give
The living water; thirsty one,
  Stoop down and drink, and live.
I came to Jesus, and I drank
  Of that life-giving stream;
My thirst was quenched, my soul revived,
  And now I live in him.

3 I heard the voice of Jesus say,
  I am this dark world's light;
Look unto me, thy morn shall rise,
  And all thy day be bright.
I looked to Jesus, and I found
  In him my star, my sun;
And in that light of life I'll walk,
  Till travelling days are done.

                                    H. BONAR.

THE CHRISTIAN LIFE.

WEBB.

258

STAND up! Stand up for Jesus!
　Ye soldiers of the cross :
Lift high the royal banner,
　It must not suffer loss.
From victory unto victory
　His army shall be led,
Till every foe is vanquish'd
　And Christ is Lord indeed.

2 Stand up! Stand up for Jesus!
　　Stand in his strength alone;
The arm of flesh will fail you—
　　Ye must not trust your own;
Put on the Gospel armor
　　And, watching unto prayer,
Where duty calls, or danger,
　　Be never wanting there.

3 Stand up! Stand up for Jesus!
　　The strife will not be long;
This day, the noise of battle,
　　The next, the victor's song,
To him that overcometh
　　A crown of life shall be—
He, with the King of glory
　　Shall reign eternally.

From Gold Chain, by permission.

THE CHRISTIAN LIFE.

ORESTES. 9th P. M.

259

VAIN are all terrestrial pleasures;
  Mix'd with dross the purest gold;
Seek we then for heavenly treasures—
  Treasures never waxing old.
Let our best affections centre
  On the things around the throne:
There no thief can ever enter;
  Moth and rust are there unknown.

2 Earthly joys no longer please us;
  Here would we renounce them all;
Seek our only rest in Jesus—
  Him our Lord and Master call.
Faith our languid spirits cheering,
  Points to brighter worlds above;
Bids us look for his appearing;
  Bids us triumph in his love.

3 May our light be always burning,
  And our loins be girded round,
Waiting for our Lord's returning—
  Longing for the welcome sound.
Thus the Christian life adorning,
  Never need we be afraid,
Should he come at night or morning,
  Early dawn or evening shade.

FORD.

OLD TUNE.   C. M. D.

260

BEHOLD I come with joy to do
  The Master's blessed will;
My Lord in outward things pursue,
  And serve his pleasure still.
Thus faithful to my Lord's commands,
  I choose the better part,
And serve with careful Martha's hands,
  But loving Mary's heart.

2 Though careful, without care I am,
  Nor feel my happy toil—
Preserved in peace by Jesus' name,
  Supported by his smile:
Rejoicing thus my faith to show,
  His service my reward;
While every work I do below,
  I do it to the Lord.

3 O! that the world the art might know,
  Of living thus to thee;
And find their Heaven begun below,
  And here thy glory see;
Walking in all the works prepared
  To exercise their grace,
They gain at last a full reward,
  To see thy glorious face.

C. WESLEY.

THE CHRISTIAN LIFE.

SICILIAN HYMN. 8th P. M.

261
GUIDE me, O thou great Jehovah,
  Pilgrim through this barren land:
I am weak, but thou art mighty;
  Hold me with thy powerful hand :
    Bread of heaven,
  Feed me till I want no more.

2 Open now the crystal fountain,
    Whence the healing waters flow;
  Let the fiery, cloudy pillar,
    Lead me all my journey through:
      Strong Deliv'rer,
    Be thou still my strength and shield.

3 When I tread the verge of Jordan,
    Bid my anxious fears subside:
  Bear me through the swelling current;
    Land me safe on Canaan's side;
      Songs of praises
    I will ever give to thee.

BARTIMEUS.

262
IN the cross of Christ I glory,
  Towering o'er the wrecks of time;
All the light of sacred story
  Gathers round its head sublime.

2 When the woes of life o'ertake me,
    Hopes deceive and fears annoy,
Never shall the Cross forsake me;
    Lo! it glows with peace and joy.

3 When the sun of bliss is beaming
    Light and love upon my way,
From the Cross the radiance streaming,
    Adds new lustre to the day.

4 Bane and blessing, pain and pleasure,
    By the Cross are sanctified;
Peace is there that knows no measure,
    Joys that through all time abide.

263

I WOULD love thee, Heavenly Father!
    My Redeemer, and my King!
I would love thee: for without thee
    Life is but a bitter thing.

2 I would love thee; every blessing
    Flows to me from out thy throne;
I would love thee; he who loves thee
    Never feels himself alone.

3 I would love thee; may thy brightness
    Dazzle my rejoicing eyes!
I would love thee; may thy goodness
    Watch from heaven o'er all I prize.

4 I will love thee, I have vowed it;
    On thy love my heart is set:
While I love thee I will never
    My Redeemer's blood forget.

THE CHRISTIAN LIFE.

THE ROYAL WAY OF THE CROSS.
Harmonium, J. P. MAGEE. Boston.

264

WE may spread our couch with roses,
    And sleep through the summer day;
But the soul that in sloth reposes
    Is not in the narrow way.
If we follow the chart that is given,
    We need not be at a loss;
For the royal way to Heaven
    Is the royal way of the cross.

2 To one who is reared in splendor,
    The cross is a heavy load;
And feet that are soft and tender,
    Will shrink from the thorny road;
But the chains of the soul must be riven,
    And wealth must be as the dross;
For the royal way to Heaven
    Is the royal way of the cross.

3 We say we will walk to-morrow,
    The path we refuse to-day,
And still, with our lukewarm sorrow,
    We shrink from the narrow way!
What heeded the chosen eleven
    How the fortunes of life might toss,
As they followed their Master to Heaven,
    By the royal way of the cross?

THORNTON. C. M. D.

265

I WANT a principle within
  Of jealous godly fear;
A sensibility of sin—
  A pain to feel it near;
I want the first approach to feel,
  Of pride, or fond desire;
To catch the wand'ring of my will,
  And quench the kindling fire.

2 From thee that I no more may part,
  No more thy goodness grieve,
The filial awe, the fleshly heart,
  The tender conscience give.
Quick as the apple of an eye,
  O God, my conscience make;
Awake my soul when sin is nigh,
  And keep it still awake.

3 If to the right or left I stray,
  That moment, Lord, reprove;
And let me weep my life away,
  For having grieved thy love.
O may the least omission pain
  My well-instructed soul,
And drive me to the blood again,
  Which makes the wounded whole.

C. WESLEY.

THE CHRISTIAN LIFE.

SWEET THE MOMENTS. 9th P. M.

266

SWEET the moments, rich in blessing,
  Which before the cross I spend;
Life and health, and peace possessing,
  From the sinner's dying friend.
Love and grief my heart dividing,
  With my tears his feet I'll bathe,
Still in faith and hope abiding—
  Life deriving from his death.

2 O how blessed is this station!
  Low before the cross I'll lie,
While I see divine compassion
  Pleading in the Victim's eye;
Here I'll sit for ever viewing,
  Mercy streaming in his blood;
Precious drops, my soul bedewing,
  Plead and claim my peace with God.

3 Here it is I find my heaven,
  While upon the Lamb I gaze;
Here I see my sins forgiven,
  Lost in wonder, love, and praise.
May I still enjoy this feeling,
  In all need to Jesus go;
Prove each day his blood more healing,
  And himself more deeply know.

PACKARD. C. M. D.

267

MY span of life will soon be done,
  The passing moments say;
As length'ning shadows o'er the mead,
  Proclaim the close of day.
O that my heart might dwell aloof
  From all created things;
And learn that wisdom from above,
  Whence true contentment springs.

2 Courage, my soul; thy bitter cross,
  In every trial here,
Shall bear thee to thy heaven above,
  But shall not enter there.
The sighing ones that humbly seek
  In sorrowing paths below,
Shall in eternity rejoice,
  Where endless comforts flow.

3 Soon will the toilsome strife be o'er,
  Of sublunary care,
And life's dull vanities no more
  This anxious breast ensnare.
Courage, my soul; on God rely;
  Deliv'rance soon will come;
A thousand ways has Providence
  To bring believers home.

MRS. COWPER.

268

GENTLY, Lord, O gently lead us
  Through this lowly vale of tears;
And do thou in love sustain us,
  Till our last great change appears.
When temptation's darts assail us,
  When in devious paths we stray,
Let thy goodness never fail us,
  Lead us in thy perfect way.

2 In the hour of pain and anguish—
  In the hour when death draws near,
Suffer not our hearts to languish—
  Suffer not our souls to fear.
And when mortal life is ended,
  Bid us in thy arms to rest,
Till, by angel-bands attended,
  We awake among the blest.

BOOTH'S S. S. HYMNS.

269

CHRISTIAN, the morn breaks sweetly o'er thee,
  And all the midnight shadows flee;
Tinged are the distant skies with glory;
  A beacon light hangs out for thee.

CHORUS.

  Arise, arise, the light breaks o'er thee,
    Thy name is graven on the throne;
  Thy home is in those worlds of glory,
    Where thy Redeemer reigns alone.

2 Thy God is ever kind and gracious;
  He will direct thy course above;
For thou art in his sight most precious,
  The object of his tender love.

3 Tossed on Time's rude, relentless surges,
  Calmly composed, and dauntless stand;
For lo, beyond those seas emerges,
  The height that bounds the promised land.

4 Christian, behold! The land is nearing,
  Where the wild sea-storm's rage is o'er;
Hark! how the heavenly hosts are cheering!
  See, in what throngs they range the shore!
                    REVIVAL & C. M. MELODIES.

EXPOSTULATION.

270

O CHRISTIAN, walk carefully; danger is near;
  And work out thy journey with trembling and fear,
The snares from without, and temptations within,
Will seek to entice thee again into sin.

2 O, Christian, walk humbly; exult not in pride;
For all that thou hast is by Jesus supplied.
He holdeth thee up, he directeth thy ways;
To him be the glory; to him be the praise.

3 O, Christian, walk cheerfully; though the dark storm
May fill thy bright sky with the clouds of alarm;
Yet soon will the clouds and the tempest be past;
And thou shalt ascend with thy Saviour at last.

HINTON.   LUTE OF ZION.

271

THE Lord is my Shepherd, no want shall I know;
   I feed in green pastures, safe-folded I rest;
He leadeth my soul where the still waters flow,
   Restores me when wand'ring, redeems when oppress'd.

2 Through the valley and shadow of death though I stray,
   Since thou art my guardian, no evil I fear;
Thy rod shall defend me, thy staff be my stay;
   No harm can befall, with my Comforter near.

3 In the midst of affliction my table is spread;
   With blessings unmeasured my cup runneth o'er;
With oil and perfume thou anointest my head;
   O, what shall I ask of thy providence more?

4 Let goodness and mercy, my bountiful God,
   Still follow my steps till I meet thee above;
I seek—by the path which my forefathers trod,
   Through the land of their sojourn—thy kingdom of love.
                                   MONTGOMERY.

272

HOW firm a foundation, ye saints of the Lord,
   Is laid for your faith, in his excellent word!
What more can he say than to you he hath said—
You who unto Jesus for refuge have fled?

2 "Fear not, I am with thee; O! be not dismayed!
   For I am thy God, and will still give thee aid;
I'll strengthen thee, help thee, and cause thee to stand,
Upheld by my righteous omnipotent hand.

3 "When through the deep waters I call thee to go,
   The rivers of woe shall not thee overflow;

For I will be with thee, in troubles to bless,
And sanctify to thee thy deepest distress.

4 "When through fiery trials thy pathway shall lie,
My grace all sufficient shall be thy supply;
The flame shall not hurt thee, I only design
Thy dross to consume, and thy gold to refine.

5 "The soul that on Jesus doth lean for repose,
I will not, I will not desert to his foes;
That soul, though all hell should endeavor to shake,
I'll never—no never—no never forsake."
ZION SONGSTER, 1833.

PORTUGUESE HYMN.

273

BEGONE, unbelief! My Saviour is near,
And for my relief will surely appear;
By prayer let me wrestle, and he will perform;
With Christ in the vessel, I smile at the storm.

2 Though dark be my way, since he is my guide,
'Tis mine to obey, 'tis his to provide:
Though cisterns be broken, and creatures all fail,
The word he has spoken shall surely prevail.

3 His love in time past forbids me to think
He'll leave me at last in troubles to sink;
Each sweet Ebenezer I have in review,
Confirms his good pleasure to bring me quite through.

4 Since all that I meet shall work for my good,
The bitter is sweet, the med'cine is food:
Though painful at present, 'twill cease before long;
And then, O how pleasant the conqueror's song.
ZION SONGSTER, 1833.

THE CHRISTIAN LIFE.

SWEET HOME.

274

'MID scenes of confusion, and creature complaints,
How sweet to my soul is communion with saints
To find at the banquet of mercy there's room,
And feel in the presence of Jesus at home.
    Home, home, sweet, sweet home,
    Prepare me, dear Saviour, for glory, my home.

2 The pleasures of earth, I have seen fade away;
They bloom for a season, but soon they decay;
But pleasures more lasting in Jesus are given—
Salvation on earth, and a mansion in Heaven.

3 Allure me no longer, ye false glowing charms!
The Saviour invites me, I'll go to his arms.
At the banquet of mercy, I hear there is room;
O there may I feast with his children at home.
                        ZION SONGSTER, 1833.

PORTUGUESE HYMN.

275

TO thee, O my Saviour, to thee will I cling;
For thou art my Lord, my Redeemer and King:
And feeling thy blessing, my spirit shall know,
Thy mercy is with me wherever I go.

2 I'm free from the anguish of doubt and despair;
I welcome the rapture of praise and of prayer;
Now, meekly confiding, in faith I rejoice
To hear the sweet tones of thy comforting voice.

THE CHRISTIAN LIFE. 217

3 Around me there shineth the heavenly ray
That scattereth clouds and their shadows away,
And melteth my soul in devotional glow;
For mercy is with me wherever I go.

4 I part with the pleasures that time can afford,
Since thou art my glory, my Saviour and Lord:
Nor fear I the darkness of death and the tomb,
Since thou art my Light in the valley of gloom.

REV. & C. M. MIN., 218.

BOWER OF PRAYER.

276

O TELL me no more of this world's vain store,
The time for such trifles with me now is o'er;
A country I've found where true joys abound;
To dwell, I'm determined, on that happy ground.

2 The souls that believe, in Paradise live;
And me in that number will Jesus receive;
My soul, don't delay—he calls thee away;
Rise, follow thy Saviour, and bless the glad day.

3 Great spoils I shall win from death, hell and sin;
'Midst outward afflictions, shall feel Christ within;
And when I'm to die, receive me, I'll cry;
For Jesus hath loved me, I cannot tell why;

4 But this I do find, we too are so joined,
He'll not live in glory, and leave me behind;
So this is the race I'm running, through grace,
Henceforth, till admitted to see my Lord's face.

NORTHFIELD. C. M.

277

WALK in the light! so shalt thou know
 That fellowship of love
His Spirit only can bestow
 Who reigns in light above.

2 Walk in the light! and thou shalt find
 Thy heart made truly His,
Who dwells in cloudless light enshrined,
 In whom no darkness is.

3 Walk in the light! and thou shalt own
 Thy darkness pass'd away,
Because that Light hath on thee shone
 In which is perfect day.

4 Walk in the light! and e'en the tomb
 No fearful shade shall wear;
Glory shall chase away its gloom,
 For Christ hath conquer'd there.

5 Walk in the light! thy path shall be
 Peaceful, serene, and bright;
For God, by grace, shall dwell in thee,
 And God himself is light.

B. BARTON.

278

I'M not ashamed to own my Lord,
 Or to defend his cause;
Maintain the honor of his word—
 The glory of his cross.

2 Jesus, my God!—I know his name;
  His name is all my trust;
Nor will he put my soul to shame,
  Nor let my hope be lost.

3 Firm as his throne his promise stands,
  And he can well secure
What I've committed to his hands,
  Till the decisive hour.

4 Then will he own my worthless name
  Before his Father's face,
And in the New Jerusalem
  Appoint my soul a place.

WATTS.

279

ALL that I was—my sin, my guilt,
  My death was all my own;
All that I am, I owe to thee,
  My gracious God alone.

2 The evil of my former state
  Was mine, and only mine;
The good in which I now rejoice,
  Is thine, and only thine.

3 Thy grace first made me feel my sin;
  It taught me to believe;
Then, in believing, peace I found;
  And now I live, I live!

4 All that I am, even here on earth,
  All that I hope to be,
When Jesus comes and glory dawns,
  I owe it, Lord, to thee.

BONAR.

220 THE CHRISTIAN LIFE.

THE CHRISTIAN HERO.
From the S. S. Bell, by permission of H. WATERS.

280

L IVE on the field of battle,
  Be earnest in the fight;
Stand forth with manly courage,
  And struggle for the right.

2 WATCH on the field of battle;
  The foe is everywhere;
His fiery darts fly thickly,
  Like lightning through the air.

3 PRAY on the field of battle;
  God works with those who pray;
His mighty arm can nerve us,
  And make us win the day.

4 DIE on the field of battle,
  'Tis noble there to die;
God smiles on valiant soldiers—
  Their record is on high.

NEVIN.

OLD WARREN.   5th P. M.

281

J ESUS, shall I never be
  Firmly grounded upon thee?
Never by thy work abide?
Never in thy wounds reside?

2 O how wav'ring is my mind,
  Toss'd about with every wind;
  O how quickly doth my heart
  From the living God depart.

3 Jesus, let my nature feel
  Thou art God unchangeable:
  JAH, JEHOVAH, great I AM,
  Speak into my soul thy Name.

4 Grant that every moment I
  May believe and feel thee nigh;
  Steadfastly behold thy face,
  'Stablish'd with abiding grace.
  C. WESLEY.

282

CHILDREN of the heavenly King,
  As we journey let us sing;
Sing our Saviour's worthy praise,
Glorious in his works and ways.

2 We are trav'ling home to God,
  In the way our fathers trod;
  They are happy now, and we
  Soon their happiness shall see.

3 Fear not, brethren, joyful stand
  On the borders of our land;
  Jesus Christ, our Father's Son,
  Bids us undismay'd go on.

4 Lord! obediently we'll go,
  Gladly leaving all below:
  Only thou our leader be,
  And we still will follow thee.
  CENNICK

THE BRIGHT CROWN.
GOLDEN CHAIN.

283

1. AM I a soldier of the cross—
A foll'wer of the Lamb—
And shall I fear to own his cause,
Or blush to speak his name?

CHORUS.
Let us never mind the scoffs nor frowns of the world,
For we all have the cross to bear;
It will only make the crown the brighter to shine,
When we have the crown to wear.

2 Must I be carried to the skies
On flowery beds of ease;
While others fought to win the prize,
And sail'd through bloody seas?

3 Are there no foes for me to face?
Must I not stem the flood?
Is this vile world a friend to grace,
To help me on to God?

4 Since I must fight if I would reign,
Increase my courage, Lord;
I'll bear the toil, endure the pain,
Supported by thy word.

5 Thy saints in all this glorious war
Shall conquer, though they die:
They see the triumph from afar—
By faith they bring it nigh.

WATTS.

THE CHRISTIAN LIFE. 223

HARWELL. 9th P. M.

284.

COME, thou all-inspiring Spirit,
  Into every longing heart!
Bought for us by Jesus' merit,
  Now thy blissful self impart:
Sign our uncontested pardon;
  Wash us in th' atoning blood:
Make our hearts a water'd garden:
  Fill our spotless souls with God.

2 Give us quietly to tarry,
   Till for all thy glory meet;
 Waiting, like attentive Mary,
   Happy at the Saviour's feet.
 Keep us from the world unspotted,
   From all earthly passions free,
 Wholly to thyself devoted,
   Fixed to live and die for thee.

3 Wrestling on in mighty prayer,
   Lord, we will not let thee go,
 Till thou all thy mind declare,
   All thy grace on us bestow:
 Peace, the seal of sin forgiven,
   Joy, and perfect love, impart,
 Present, everlasting heaven,
   All thou hast and all thou art.

C. WESLEY.

THE CHRISTIAN LIFE.

WOODLAND.

285

AWAKE, my soul! stretch every nerve,
   And press with vigor on;
A heavenly race demands thy zeal,
   And an immortal crown.

2 'Tis God's all-animating voice
   That calls thee from on high;
'Tis he whose hand presents the prize
   To thine aspiring eye.

3 A cloud of witnesses around
   Hold thee in full survey;
Forget the steps already trod,
   And onward urge thy way.

4 Blest Saviour! introduced by thee,
   Our race have we begun;
And, crown'd with vict'ry, at thy feet
   We'll lay our trophies down.
                                        DODDRIDGE.

286

WHEN I can read my title clear
   To mansions in the skies,
I'll bid farewell to every fear,
   And wipe my weeping eyes.

2 Should earth against my soul engage,
   And fiery darts be hurl'd,
Then I can smile at Satan's rage,
   And face a frowning world.

3 Let cares like a wild deluge come,
  Let storms of sorrow fall,
So I but safely reach my home,
  My God, my heaven, my all.

4 There I shall bathe my weary soul,
  In seas of heavenly rest,
And not a wave of trouble roll
  Across my peaceful breast.

WATTS.

ST. THOMAS.   S. M.

287

MY soul, be on thy guard;
  Ten thousand foes arise;
The hosts of sin are pressing hard
  To draw thee from the skies.

2 O watch, and fight, and pray;
  The battle ne'er give o'er;
Renew it boldly every day,
  And help divine implore.

3 Ne'er think the vict'ry won,
  Nor lay thine armor down:
The work of faith will not be done,
  Till thou obtain the crown.

4 Then persevere till death
  Shall bring thee to thy God;
He'll take thee, at thy parting breath,
  To his divine abode.

HEATH.

226 THE CHRISTIAN LIFE.

CROSS AND CROWN. C. M.

288
MUST Jesus bear the cross alone,
    And all the world go free?
No! there's a cross for every one,
    And there's a cross for me.

2 How happy are the saints above,
    Who once went sorrowing here;
But now they taste unmingled love,
    And joy without a tear.

3 The consecrated cross I'll bear,
    Till death shall set me free;
And then go home a crown to wear,
    For there's a crown for me.

GOLDEN HILL.

289
EQUIP me for the war,
    And teach my hands to fight;
My simple, upright heart prepare,
    And guide my words aright.

2 Control my every thought:
    My whole of sin remove:
Let all my works in thee be wrought;
    Let all be wrought in love.

THE CHRISTIAN LIFE. 227

3 O arm me with the mind,
  Meek Lamb, that was in thee;
And let my knowing zeal be join'd
  With perfect charity.

4 With calm and temper'd zeal
  Let me enforce thy call:
And vindicate thy gracious will,
  Which offers life to all.

C. WESLEY.

RETREAT. L. M.

290

GOD leadeth me! O blessed thought!
  Through deserts drear, with dangers fraught:
Whate'er I do, where'er I be,
'Tis God's own hand that leadeth me.

2 Sometimes 'mid scenes of deepest gloom,
  Sometimes where Eden's bowers bloom,
By waters still, o'er troubled sea,
Still 'tis his hand that leadeth me!

3 Lord, I would clasp thy hand in mine,
  Nor ever murmur nor repine—
Content, whatever lot I see,
Since 'tis my God that leadeth me.

4 And when my task on earth is done,
  When, by thy grace, the victory's won,
E'en death's cold grave I will not flee,
Since God through Jordan leadeth me.

ANON.

FOREST.   L. M.

291

WHEN I survey the wondrous cross
  On which the Prince of glory died,
My richest gain I count but loss,
  And pour contempt on all my pride.

2 Forbid it, Lord, that I should boast,
  Save in the death of Christ, my God;
All the vain things that charm me most,
  I sacrifice them to his blood.

3 See, from his head, his hands, his feet,
  Sorrow and love flow mingled down:
Did e'er such love and sorrow meet,
  Or thorns compose so rich a crown.

4 Were the whole realm of nature mine,
  That were a present far too small;
Love so amazing, so divine,
  Demands my soul, my life, my all.
                        WATTS.

292

SHALL I, for fear of feeble man,
  The Spirit's course in me restrain?
Or, undismay'd in deed and word,
Be a true witness of my Lord?

2 Awed by a mortal's frown, shall I
Conceal the word of God Most High?
How then before thee shall I dare
To stand, or how thine anger bear?

3 Shall I, to soothe the' unholy throng,
Soften thy truth, or smooth my tongue,
To gain earth's gilded toys, or flee
The cross endured, my Lord, by thee?

4 What then is he whose scorn I dread?
Whose wrath or hate makes me afraid?
A man! an heir of death! a slave
To sin! a bubble on the wave!

5 Yea, let men rage; since thou wilt spread
Thy shadowing wings around my head:
Since in all pain thy tender love
Will still my sure refreshment prove.

J. WESLEY.

NORRIS.  L. M.

293

LORD, fill me with an humble fear;
    My utter helplessness reveal;
Satan and sin are always near—
    Thee may I always nearer feel.

2 O that to thee my constant mind
    Might with an even flame aspire;
Pride in its earliest motions find,
    And mark the risings of desire.

3 O that my tender soul might fly
    The first abhorr'd approach of ill;
Quick as the apple of an eye,
    The slightest touch of sin to feel.

C. WESLEY.

THE CHRISTIAN LIFE.

BRIGHTON. 1st P. M.

294

WHEN gathering clouds around I view,
  And days are dark and friends are few,
On him I lean, who not in vain
Experienced every human pain;
He feels my griefs, he sees my fears,
And counts and treasures up my tears.

2 If aught should tempt my soul to stray
From heavenly virtue's narrow way—
To fly the good I should pursue,
Or do the sin I should not do;
Still he who felt temptation's power,
Shall guard me in that dangerous hour.

3 And, O, when I have safely past
Through every conflict but the last,
Still, still unchanging, watch beside
My bed of death, for thou hast died!
Then point to realms of cloudless day,
And wipe the latest tear away.

SCOTCH MELODY. MASON'S NORMAL SINGER.

295

I WANT to live near Jesus,
  And never go astray;

To feel that I am growing
  More like him every day:
That I am always laying,
  My treasure up above;
And gaining more the spirit,
  Of gentleness and love.

2 I want such steadfast purpose,
   My mission to fulfil;
 That it may be my meat and drink,
   To do my Father's will.
 To follow in his footsteps,
   Who never turned aside—
 From the path that leads to Heaven,
   Though often sorely tried.

3 Oh! that in his humility,
   My spirit may be clad!
 That I may have the patience
   My suffering Saviour had.
 A heart more disengaged,
   From earth and earthly things;
 Which through life's varied trials,
   To Jesus simply clings.

4 Oh! I shall live near Jesus,
   And never go astray;
 And every sinful stain
   Shall soon be washed away;
 And I'll bear my master's image,
   When I see him face to face;
 Then earth shall lose the power,
   Its brightness to efface.

VIII.—CONSECRATION & HOLINESS.

PETERBORO'.   C. M.

296

O FOR a heart to praise my God,
  A heart from sin set free;
A heart that always feels thy blood,
  So freely spilt for me:

2 A heart resign'd, submissive, meek,
  My great Redeemer's throne;
Where only Christ is heard to speak—
  Where Jesus reigns alone.

3 A heart in every thought renew'd,
  And full of love divine;
Perfect, and right, and pure, and good,
  A copy, Lord, of thine.

4 Thy nature, gracious Lord, impart;
  Come quickly from above;
Write thy new name upon my heart—
  Thy new, best name of Love.   C. WESLEY.

297

FOREVER here my rest shall be,
  Close to thy bleeding side;
This all my hope, and all my plea—
  For me the Saviour died.

2 My dying Saviour, and my God,
  Fountain for guilt and sin,
Sprinkle me ever with thy blood,
  And cleanse and keep me clean.

3 Wash me, and make me thus thine own;
  Wash me, and mine thou art;
Wash me, but not my feet alone—
  My hands, my head, my heart.

4 The' atonement of thy blood apply,
  Till faith to sight improve;
Till hope in full fruition die,
  And all my soul be love.

C. WESLEY.

WARWICK.   C. M.

298

LET Him to whom we now belong,
  His sov'reign right assert;
And take up every thankful song,
  And every loving heart.

2 He justly claims us for his own,
  Who bought us with a price:
The Christian lives to Christ alone;
  To Christ alone he dies.

3 Jesus, thine own at last receive;
  Fulfil our heart's desire;
And let us to thy glory live,
  And in thy cause expire.

4 Our souls and bodies we resign;
  With joy we render thee
Our all—no longer ours, but thine
  To all eternity.

C. WESLEY.

234 CONSECRATION AND HOLINESS.

CARMARTHEN. 3d P. M.

299

IN God we put our trust;
  If we our sins confess,
Faithful is he and just,
  From all unrighteousness
To cleanse us all, both you and me:
We shall from all our sins be free.

2 Who Jesus' suff'rings share,
    My fellow-pris'ners now,
  Ye soon the crown shall wear
    On your triumphant brow:
  Rejoice in hope, rejoice with me;
  We shall from all our sins be free.

3 The word of God is sure,
    And never can remove;
  We shall in heart be pure,
    And perfected in love:
  Rejoice in hope, rejoice with me;
  We shall from all our sins be free.

4 Then let us gladly bring
    Our sacrifice of praise:
  Let us give thanks and sing,
    And glory in his grace:
  Rejoice in hope, rejoice with me;
  We shall from all our sins be free.

C. WESLEY.

CONSECRATION AND HOLINESS. 235

NUREMBURG. 6th P. M.

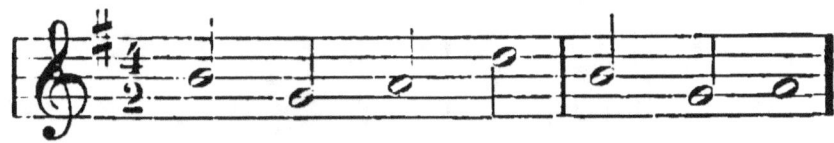

300

FATHER, Son, and Holy Ghost,
  One in Three, and Three in One,
As by the celestial host,
  Let thy will on earth be done;
Praise by all to thee be given,
Glorious Lord of earth and heaven.

2 Vilest of the sinful race,
    Lo! I answer to thy call:
  Meanest vessel of thy grace,
    Grace divinely free for all;
  Lo! I come to do thy will,
  All thy counsel to fulfil.

3 If so poor a worm as I
    May to thy great glory live,
  All my actions sanctify,
    All my words and thoughts receive;
  Claim me for thy service, claim
  All I have, and all I am.

4 Take my soul and body's powers;
    Take my mem'ry, mind, and will;
  All my goods, and all my hours;
    All I know, and all I feel;
  All I think, or speak, or do;
  Take my heart, but make it new.

C. WESLEY.

CONSECRATION AND HOLINESS.

DISCIPLE.   9th P. M.

301

JESUS, I my cross have taken,
   All to leave and follow thee:
Naked, poor, despised, forsaken,
   Thou, from hence, my all shalt be.
Perish, every fond ambition;
   All I've sought, or hoped, or known:
Yet how rich is my condition;
   God and heaven are still my own!

2 Soul, then know thy full salvation;
   Rise o'er sin, and fear, and care;
Joy to find in every station
   Something still to do or bear.
Think what Spirit dwells within thee;
   Think what Father's smiles are thine,
Think that Jesus died to win thee;
   Child of heaven, canst thou repine?

3 Haste thee on from grace to glory,
   Armed by faith, and winged by prayer;
Heaven's eternal day's before thee,
   God's own hand shall guide thee there.
Soon shall close thy earthly mission,
   Soon shall pass thy pilgrim days;
Hope shall change to glad fruition,
   Faith to sight, and prayer to praise.

HARWELL. 9th P. M.

302

SAVIOUR, while my heart is tender,
  I would yield that heart to thee;
All my powers to thee surrender,
  Thine, and only thine, to be.
Take me now, Lord Jesus, take me;
  Let my trusting heart be thine;
Thy devoted servant make me;
  Fill my soul with love divine.

2 Send me, Lord, where thou wilt send me,
    Only do thou guide the way;
  May thy grace through life attend me,
    Gladly then shall I obey.
  Let me do thy will, or bear it,
    I would know no will but thine;
  Shouldst thou take my life, or spare it,
    I that life to thee resign.

3 May this solemn dedication
    Never once forgotten lie;
  Let it know no revocation,
    Published and confirmed on high.
  Thine I am, O Lord, forever,
    To thy service set apart;
  Suffer me to leave thee never;
    Seal thy image on my heart.

CONSECRATION AND HOLINESS.

DUANE STREET. L. M. D.

303

JESUS, my all, to heaven is gone—
He whom I fix my hopes upon;
His track I see, and I'll pursue
The narrow way, till him I view;
The way the holy prophets went—
The road that leads from banishment—
The King's highway of holiness,
I'll go, for all his paths are peace.

2 This is the way I long have sought,
And mourn'd because I found it not;
My grief a burden long has been,
Because I was not saved from sin;
The more I strove against its power,
I felt its weight and guilt the more;
Till late I heard my Saviour say—
Come hither, soul, I am the way.

3 Lo! glad I come; and thou, blest Lamb,
Shalt take me to thee, as I am:
Nothing but sin have I to give—
Nothing but love shall I receive;
Then will I tell to sinners round,
What a dear Saviour I have found;
I'll point to thy redeeming blood,
And say—Behold the way to God.

C. WESLEY.

CONSECRATION AND HOLINESS.

REST.   L. M.

304

REST for my soul I long to find:
  Saviour of all, if mine thou art,
Give me thy meek and lowly mind,
  And stamp thine image on my heart.

2 Break off the yoke of inbred sin,
  And fully set my spirit free;
I cannot rest till pure within—
  Till I am wholly lost in thee.

3 Fain would I learn of thee, my God;
  Thy light and easy burden prove;
The cross all stain'd with hallow'd blood,
  The labor of thy dying love.

4 I would, but thou must give the power;
  My heart from every sin release;
Bring near, bring near the joyful hour,
  And fill me with thy perfect peace.
                                  C. WESLEY.

305

WHAT! never speak one evil word?
  Or rash, or idle, or unkind?
O how shall I, most gracious Lord,
  This mark of true perfection find?

2 Thy sinless mind in me reveal;
  Thy Spirit's plenitude impart;
And all my spotless life shall tell
  The' abundance of a loving heart.
                                  C. WESLEY

240 CONSECRATION AND HOLINESS.

PLYMOUTH DOCK.   1st P. M.

306

COME, Holy Ghost, all-quick'ning fire,
  Come, and in me delight to rest;
Drawn by the lure of strong desire,
  O come and consecrate my breast;
The temple of my soul prepare,
And fix thy sacred presence there.

2 If now thine influence I feel,
  If now in thee begin to live,
Still to my heart thyself reveal;
  Give me thyself, forever give:
A point my good, a drop my store,
Eager I ask, I pant for more.

3 Eager for thee I ask and pant,
  So strong the principle divine
Carries me out with sweet constraint,
  Till all my hallow'd soul is thine;
Plunged in the Godhead's deepest sea,
And lost in thy immensity.

4 My peace, my life, my comfort thou,
  My treasure and my all thou art;
True witness of my sonship, now
  Engraving pardon on my heart:
Seal of my sins in Christ forgiven,
Earnest of love, and pledge of heaven.
C. WESLEY.

CONSECRATION AND HOLINESS.

BRIGHTON. 1st P. M.

307

O GOD, what off'ring shall I give
 To thee, the Lord of earth and skies?
My spirit, soul, and flesh receive,
 A holy, living sacrifice:
Small as it is, 'tis all my store;
More shouldst thou have, if I had more.

2 Now, then, my God, thou hast my soul:
 No longer mine, but thine I am:
Guard thou thine own, possess it whole;
 Cheer it with hope, with love inflame.
Thou hast my spirit; there display
Thy glory to the perfect day.

3 Thou hast my flesh, thy hallow'd shrine,
 Devoted solely to thy will:
Here let thy light forever shine;
 This house still let thy presence fill.
O Source of life! live, dwell, and move
In me, till all my life is love.

4 Lord, arm me with thy Spirit's might:
 Since I am call'd by thy great name,
In thee let all my thoughts unite;
 Of all my works be thou the aim:
Thy love attend me all my days,
And my sole business be thy praise.

J. WESLEY.

CONSECRATION AND HOLINESS.

GIVE. C. M.

308

1. I WANT to live, as one who knows
The fellowship of love;
As one whose eyes can pierce beyond
The pearl-built gates above.

2. I want to walk as one who knows
The guilt that lurks within;
Yet trusts in humble faith that blood
Which cleanses from all sin.

3. To dwell more near my Saviour's face,
Than ever yet before;
To lean upon his loving breast,
And own him CONQUEROR.

4. Lord, I desire to live as one
Who bears a blood-bought name;
As one who fears but grieving thee,
And knows no other shame;

5. As one by whom thy walk below
Should never be forgot;
As one who fain would keep apart,
From all thou lovest not.

6. As one who daily speaks to thee,
And hears thy voice divine,
With depths of tenderness declare:
"Beloved! thou art mine."

CONSECRATION AND HOLINESS. 243

MADRID. 9th P. M.

309

YE who know your sins forgiven,
   And are happy in the Lord,
Have ye read that gracious promise,
   Which is left upon record?—
" I will sprinkle you with water;
   I will cleanse you from all sin;
Sanctify and make you holy;
   I will dwell and reign within. "

2 Though you have much peace and comfort,
   Greater things you yet may find;
Freedom from unholy tempers,
   Freedom from the carnal mind.
To procure your perfect freedom,
   Jesus suffered, groaned, and died—
On the cross the healing fountain
   Gushed from his wounded side.

3 Be as holy and as happy,
   And as useful here below,
As it is your Father's pleasure:
   Jesus, only Jesus know.
Spread, O spread the holy fire;
   Tell, O tell what God has done,
Till the nations are conformed
   To the image of his Son.

ZION SONGSTER, 1833.

CONSECRATION AND HOLINESS.

WATCHMAN. S. M.

310

THE thing my God doth hate,
  That I no more may do,
Thy creature, Lord, again create,
  And all my soul renew.

2 My soul shall then, like thine,
  Abhor the thing unclean,
And, sanctified by love divine,
  Forever cease from sin.

3 That blessed law of thine,
  Jesus, to me impart—
The Spirit's law of life divine—
  O write it in my heart!

4 Implant it deep within,
  Whence it may ne'er remove—
The law of liberty from sin,
  The perfect law of love.

5 Thy nature be my law,—
  Thy spotless sanctity;
And sweetly every moment draw
  My happy soul to thee.

6 Soul of my soul, remain!
  Who didst for all fulfil,
In me, O Lord, fulfil again,
  Thy heavenly Father's will.

C. WESLEY.

OLMUTZ. S. M.

311

O COME and dwell in me.
  Spirit of power within;
And bring the glorious liberty
  From sorrow, fear, and sin!

2 Hasten the joyful day
  Which shall my sins consume;
When old things shall be done away,
  And all things new become.

3 I want the witness, Lord,
  That all I do is right,—
According to thy will and word,—
  Well pleasing in thy sight.

4 I ask no higher state;
  Indulge me but in this,
And soon or later then translate
  To my eternal bliss.

C. WESLEY.

312

CALL'D from above, I rise,
  And wash away my sin;
The stream to which my spirit flies,
  Can make the foulest clean.

2 It runs divinely clear,
  A fountain deep and wide:
'Twas opened by the soldier's spear,
  In my Redeemer's side.

KEBLE.

CONSECRATION AND HOLINESS.

THE GARDEN HYMN. 4th P. M.

313

1. O GLORIOUS hope of perfect love,
It lifts me up to things above;
 It bears on eagles' wings;
It gives my ravish'd soul a taste,
And makes me for some moments feast
 With Jesus' priests and kings.

2 Rejoicing now in earnest hope,
I stand, and from the mountain top
 See all the land below:
Rivers of milk and honey rise,
And all the fruits of paradise
 In endless plenty grow.

3 A land of corn, and wine, and oil,
Favor'd with God's peculiar smile,
 With every blessing blest;
There dwells the Lord our Righteousness,
And keeps his own in perfect peace,
 And everlasting rest.

4 O that I might at once go up;
No more on this side Jordan stop,
 But now the land possess;
This moment end my legal years,
Sorrows and sins, and doubts and fears,
 A howling wilderness.

C. WESLEY.

CONSECRATION AND HOLINESS. 247

WILLOUGHBY. 4th P. M.

314

O LOVE divine, how sweet thou art!
  When shall I find my willing heart
    All taken up by thee?
I thirst, I faint, I die to prove
The greatness of redeeming love,—
  The love of Christ to me.

2. God only knows the love of God;
  O that it now were shed abroad
    In this poor stony heart:
For love I sigh, for love I pine;
This only portion, Lord, be mine;
  Be mine this better part.

3 O that I could for ever sit
  With Mary at the Master's feet!
    Be this my happy choice;
My only care, delight and bliss,
My joy, my heaven on earth, be this,
  To hear the Bridegroom's voice.

4 O that I could, with favor'd John,
  Recline my weary head upon
    The dear Redeemer's breast:
From care, and sin, and sorrow free,
Give me, O Lord, to find in thee
  My everlasting rest.
                          C. WESLEY.

CONSECRATION AND HOLINESS.

WARE. L. M.

315
C OME, Saviour, Jesus, from above,
   Assist me with thy heavenly grace;
Empty my heart of earthly love,
   And for thyself prepare the place.

2 O let thy sacred presence fill,
   And set my longing spirit free;
Which pants to have no other will,
   But night and day to feast on thee.

3 While in this region here below,
   No other good will I pursue:
I'll bid this world of noise and show,
   With all its glitt'ring snares, adieu.

4 That path with humble speed I'll seek,
   In which my Saviour's footsteps shine,
Nor will I hear, nor will I speak,
   Of any other love but thine.
                                C. WESLEY.

316
O GOD, most merciful and true,
  Thy nature to my soul impart;
'Stablish with me the cov'nant new,
  And stamp thine image on my heart.

2 To real holiness restored,
   O let me gain my Saviour's mind;
And in the knowledge of my Lord,
   Fulness of life eternal find.

CONSECRATION AND HOLINESS. 249

3 Remember, Lord, my sins no more,
    That them I may no more forget;
  But, sunk in guiltless shame, adore,
    With speechless wonder, at thy feet.

4 O'erwhelm'd with thy stupendous grace,
    I shall not in thy presence move;
  But breathe unutterable praise,
    And rapt'rous awe, and silent love.
                                        C. WESLEY.

SESSIONS.   L. M.

317

LORD, I am thine, entirely thine,
  Purchased and saved by blood divine;
With full consent thine would I be,
And own thy sov'reign right in me.

2 Thine would I live, thine would I die;
  Be thine through all eternity;
  The vow is past beyond repeal,
  And now I set the solemn seal.

3 Here, at that cross where flows the blood
  That bought my guilty soul for God,—
  Thee, my new Master, now I call,
  And consecrate to thee my all.

4 Do thou assist a feeble worm
    The great engagement to perform;
  Thy grace can full assistance lend,
  And on that grace I dare depend.
                                        DAVIES.

250 CONSECRATION AND HOLINESS.

OLD HUNDRED. L. M.

318

COME, O thou greater than our heart,
  And make thy faithful mercies known;
The mind which was in thee impart:
  Thy constant mind in us be shown.

2 O let us by thy cross abide,
  Thee, only thee, resolved to know,
The Lamb for sinners crucified,
  A world to save from endless wo.

3 Take us into thy people's rest,
  And we from our own works shall cease;
With thy meek Spirit arm our breast,
  And keep our minds in perfect peace.

4 Jesus, for this we calmly wait;
  O let our eyes behold thee near!
Hasten to make our heaven complete;
  Appear, our glorious God, appear.
C. WESLEY.

319

O THOU, to whose all-searching sight
  The darkness shineth as the light,
Search, prove my heart, it pants for thee;
O burst these bonds, and set it free.

2 Wash out its stains, refine its dross;
Nail my affections to the cross;
Hallow each thought; let all within
Be clean, as thou, my Lord, art clean.

3 Saviour, where'er thy steps I see,
Dauntless, untired I follow thee;
O let thy hand support me still,
And lead me to thy holy hill.

4 If rough and thorny be the way,
My strength proportion to my day;
Till toil, and grief, and pain shall cease,
Where all is calm, and joy, and peace.

J. WESLEY.

DUKE STREET.   L. M.

320

I THIRST, thou wounded Lamb of God,
To wash me in thy cleansing blood;
To dwell within thy wounds; then pain
Is sweet, and life or death is gain.

2 Take my poor heart, and let it be
Forever closed to all but thee:
Seal thou my breast, and let me wear
That pledge of love for ever there.

3 How can it be, thou heavenly King,
That thou shouldst us to glory bring;
Make slaves the partners of thy throne,
Deck'd with a never-fading crown?

4 Hence our hearts melt, our eyes o'erflow,
Our words are lost, nor will we know,
Nor will we think of aught beside—
My Lord, my Love, is crucified.

J. WESLEY

CONSECRATION AND HOLINESS.

ROCKPORT.   12th P. M.

221

EVER fainting with desire,
  For thee, O Christ, I call;
Thee I restlessly require;
  I want my God, my all.
Jesus, dear redeeming Lord,
  I wait thy coming from above;
Help me, Saviour, speak the word,
  And perfect me in love.

2 Wilt thou suffer me to go
    Lamenting all my days?
  Shall I never, never know
    Thy sanctifying grace?
  Wilt thou not thy light afford?
    The darkness from my soul remove?
  Help me, Saviour, speak the word,
    And perfect me in love.

3 Thou my life, my treasure be,
    My portion here below:
  Nothing would I seek but thee,—
    Thee only would I know;
  My exceeding great reward,—
    My heaven on earth, my heaven above;
  Help me, Saviour, speak the word,
    And perfect me in love.

C. WESLEY.

CONSECRATION AND HOLINESS. 253

GREENVILLE. 9th P. M.

322

LOVE divine, all love excelling,
  Joy of heaven, to earth come down,
Fix in us thy humble dwelling;
  All thy faithful mercies crown.
Jesus, thou art all compassion—
  Pure unbounded love thou art;
Visit us with thy salvation:
  Enter every trembling heart.

2 Breathe, O breathe thy loving Spirit
    Into every troubled breast;
  Let us all in thee inherit;
    Let us find that second rest.
  Take away our bent to sinning:
    Alpha and Omega be;
  End of faith, as its beginning,
    Set our hearts at liberty.

3 Finish then thy new creation;
    Pure and spotless let us be;
  Let us see thy great salvation,
    Perfectly restored in thee;
  Changed from glory into glory,
    Till in heaven we take our place—
  Till we cast our crowns before thee,
    Lost in wonder, love and praise.

C. WESLEY.

254 CONSECRATION AND HOLINESS.

BALERMA. C. M.

323

WHAT is our calling's glorious hope,
  But inward holiness?
For this to Jesus I look up:
  I calmly wait for this.

2 I wait till he shall touch me clean—
  Shall life and power impart;
Give me the faith that casts out sin,
  And purifies the heart.

3 When Jesus makes my heart his home,
  My sin shall all depart;
And, lo! he saith, I quickly come,
  To fill and rule thy heart.

4 Be it according to thy word;
  Redeem me from all sin;
My heart would now receive thee, Lord;
  Come in, my Lord, come in!

C. WESLEY.

324

BEING of beings, God of love,
  To thee our hearts we raise:
Thy all-sustaining power we prove,
  And gladly sing thy praise.

2 Thine, wholy thine, we pant to be;
  Our sacrifice receive:
Made, and preserved, and saved by thee,
  To thee ourselves we give.

3 Heavenward our every wish aspires,
   For all thy mercy's store;
 The sole return thy love requires,
   Is that we ask for more.

4 For more we ask; we open then
   Our hearts to' embrace thy will;
 Turn, and revive us, Lord, again;
   With all thy fulness fill.

C. WESLEY.

MEAR.   C. M.

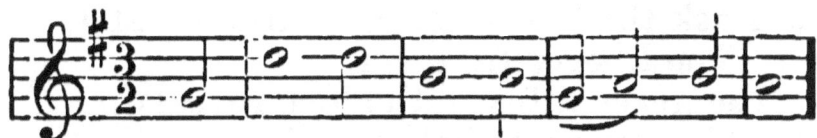

325

JESUS, thine all-victorious love
   Shed in my heart abroad:
 Then shall my feet no longer rove,
   Rooted and fix'd in God.

2 O that in me the sacred fire
   Might now begin to glow;
 Burn up the dross of base desire,
   And make the mountains flow.

3 O that it now from heaven might fall,
   And all my sins consume;
 Come, Holy Ghost, for thee I call;
   Spirit of burning, come.

4 Refining fire, go through my heart;
   Illuminate my soul;
 Scatter thy life through every part,
   And sanctify the whole.

C. WESLEY.

CONSECRATION AND HOLINESS.

GIVE. C. M.

326

1 I ASK the gift of righteousness,
  The sin-subduing power;
Power to believe, and go in peace,
  And never grieve thee more.

2 I ask the blood-bought pardon seal'd,
  The liberty from sin,
The grace infused, the love reveal'd,
  The kingdom fix'd within.

3 My restless soul cries out, oppress'd,
  Impatient to be freed;
Nor can I, Lord, nor will I rest,
  Till I am saved indeed.

4 Thou canst, thou wilt, I dare believe,
  So arm me with thy power,
That I to sin may never cleave,—
  May never feel it more.

C. WESLEY.

327

1 I WANT thy life, thy purity,
  Thy righteousness, brought in:
I ask, desire, and trust in thee
  To be redeem'd from sin.

2 For this, as taught by thee, I pray,
  My inbred sin cast out:
Thou wilt, in me, thy power display;
  I can no longer doubt.

CONSECRATION AND HOLINESS.

3 Saviour, to thee my soul looks up,
  My present Saviour thou!
In all the confidence of hope,
  I claim the blessing now.

4 'Tis done; thou dost this moment save,
  With full salvation bless;
Redemption through thy blood I have,
  And spotless love and peace.

C. WESLEY.

DOWNS. C. M.

328

JESUS hath died that I might live,
  Might live to God alone;
In him eternal life receive,
  And be in spirit one.

2 My soul breaks out in strong desire,
  The perfect bliss to prove;
My longing heart is all on fire
  To be dissolved in love.

3 Give me thyself; from every boast,
  From every wish set free;
Let all I am in thee be lost,
  But give thyself to me.

4 Thy gifts, alas! can not suffice,
  Unless thyself be given;
Thy presence makes my paradise,
  And where thou art is heaven.

C. WESLEY.

258 CONSECRATION AND HOLINESS.

WILMOT. 5th P. M.

329

JESUS comes with all his grace,
 Comes to save a fallen race;
Object of our glorious hope,
Jesus comes to lift us up.

2 Let the living stones cry out;
Let the sons of Abrah'm shout:
Praise we all our lowly King;
Give him thanks, rejoice, and sing.

3 We are now his lawful right;
Walk as children of the light;
We shall soon obtain the grace,
Pure in heart, to see his face.

4 Hasten, Lord, the perfect day;
Let thy every servant say—
I have now obtain'd the power,
Born of God, to sin no more.
 C. WESLEY.

330

SAVIOUR of the sin-sick soul,
 Give me faith to make me whole;
Finish thy great work of grace;
Cut it short in righteousness.

2 Speak the second time—Be clean!
Take away my inbred sin!
Every stumbling-block remove;
Cast it out by perfect love.

3 Nothing less will I require;
Nothing more can I desire:
None but Christ to me be given;
None but Christ in earth or heaven.

4 O that I might now decrease!
O that all I am might cease!
Let me into nothing fall;
Let my Lord be all in all!

C. WESLEY.

OLD WARREN. 5th P. M.

331

PRINCE of peace, control my will;
Bid this struggling heart be still;
Bid my fears and doubtings cease—
Hush my spirit into peace.

2 Thou hast bought me with thy blood,
Open'd wide the gate to God:
Peace I ask, but peace must be,
Lord, in being one with thee.

3 May thy will, not mine, be done;
May thy will and mine be one;
Chase these doubtings from my heart;
Now thy perfect peace impart.

4 Saviour! at thy feet I fall;
Thou my life, my God, my all!
Let thy happy servant be
One for evermore with thee!

METH. HYMN.

CONSECRATION AND HOLINESS.

ORTONVILLE. C. M.

332
LET worldly minds the world pursue;
  It has no charm for me:
Once I admired its trifles too,
  But grace hath set me free.

2 Its pleasures can no longer please,
  Nor happiness afford:
Far from my heart be joys like these,
  Now I have seen the Lord.

3 As by the light of opening day
  The stars are all conceal'd,
So earthly pleasures fade away,
  When Jesus is reveal'd.

4 Creatures no more divide my choice;
  I bid them all depart:
His name, his love, his gracious voice,
  Have fix'd my roving heart.
                      NEWTON.

333
IF thou impart thyself to me,
  No other good I need:
If thou, the Son, shalt make me free,
  I shall be free indeed.

2 I cannot rest till in thy blood
  I full redemption have;
But thou, through whom I come to God,
  Canst to the utmost save.

CONSECRATION AND HOLINESS. 261

3 From sin—the guilt, the power, the pain,
  Thou wilt redeem my soul:
Lord, I believe, and not in vain;
  My faith shall make me whole.

4 I, too, with thee, shall walk in white;
  With all thy saints shall prove [height
The length and depth, and breadth and
  Of everlasting love.

C. WESLEY.

SWANWICK.   C. M.

334

LORD, I believe a rest remains
  To all thy people known;
A rest where pure enjoyment reigns,
  And thou art loved alone:

2 A rest where all our soul's desire
  Is fix'd on things above;
Where fear, and sin, and grief expire,
  Cast out by perfect love.

3 O that I now the rest might know,
  Believe, and enter in:
Now, Saviour, now the power bestow,
  And let me cease from sin.

4 Remove this hardness from my heart;
  This unbelief remove:
To me the rest of faith impart—
  The Sabbath of thy love.

C. WESLEY.

262 CONSECRATION AND HOLINESS.

RETREAT. L. M.

235
HOLY, and true, and righteous Lord,
I wait to prove thy perfect will:
Be mindful of thy gracious word,
And stamp me with thy Spirit's seal.

2 Open my faith's interior eye:
Display thy glory from above;
And all I am shall sink and die,
Lost in astonishment and love.

3 Confound, o'erpower me by thy grace;
I would be by myself abhorr'd;
All might, all majesty, all praise,
All glory, be to Christ, my Lord.

4 Now let me gain perfection's height;
Now let me into nothing fall,
As less than nothing in thy sight,
And feel that Christ is all in all.
C. WESLEY.

336
THY loving Spirit, Lord, alone,
Can lead me forth, and make me free;
The bondage break in which I groan,
And set my heart at liberty.

2 Now let thy Spirit bring me in,
And give thy servant to possess
The land of rest from inbred sin—
The land of perfect holiness.

3 Lord, I believe thy power the same;
  The same thy truth and grace endure;
And in thy blessed hands I am,
  And trust thee for a perfect cure.

4 Come, Saviour, come, and make me whole;
  Entirely all my sins remove;
To perfect health restore my soul—
  To perfect holiness and love.
                              C. WESLEY

HEBRON.   L. M.

337

JESUS, our best beloved friend,
  Draw out our souls in sweet desire;
Jesus, in love to us descend—
  Baptize us with thy Spirit's fire.

2 On thy redeeming name we call,
    Poor and unworthy though we be;
  Pardon and sanctify us all—
    Let each thy full salvation see.

3 Our souls and bodies we resign,
    To fear and follow thy commands;
  O take our hearts, our hearts are thine;
    Accept the service of our hands.

4 Firm, faithful, watching unto prayer,
    Our Master's voice will we obey;
  Toil in the vineyard here, and bear
    The heat and burden of the day.
                              MONTGOMERY.

CONSECRATION AND HOLINESS.

ARLINGTON. C. M.

338
JESUS, the sinner's rest thou art,
From guilt, and fear, and pain;
While thou are absent from the heart
We look for rest in vain.

2 O when wilt thou my Saviour be?
O when shall I be clean?
The true eternal Sabbath see—
A perfect rest from sin?

3 I look to my incarnate God
Till he his work begin;
And wait till his redeeming blood
Shall cleanse me from all sin.

4 O that I now the voice might hear
That speaks my sins forgiven;
Thy word is pass'd to give me here
The inward pledge of heaven.

TOPLADY.

339
I LIFT mine eyes to thee,
Thou gracious, bleeding Lamb,
That I may now enlighten'd be,
And never put to shame.

2 Never will I remove
Out of thy hands my cause;
But rest in thy redeeming love,
And hang upon thy cross.

CONSECRATION AND HOLINESS. 265

3 O make me all like thee,
  Before I hence remove;
Settle, confirm, and 'stablish me,
  And build me up in love.

4 Let me thy witness live,
  When sin is all destroy'd;
And then my spotless soul receive,
  And take me home to God.
      C. WESLEY.

BALERMA. C. M.

340

DEEPEN the wound thy hands have made
  In this weak helpless soul:
Till mercy, with its balmy aid,
  Descend to make me whole.

2 The sharpness of thy two-edged sword
  Enable me to' endure;
Till bold to say—My hall'wing Lord
  Hath wrought a perfect cure.

3 I see the' exceeding broad command,
  Which all contains in one:
Enlarge my heart to understand
  The mystery unknown.

4 O that, with all thy saints, I might
  By sweet experience prove
What is the length, and breadth, and height,
  And depth, of perfect love.
      C. WESLEY.

CONSECRATION AND HOLINESS.

HORTON. 5th P. M.

341

HOLY Lamb, who thee receive,
Who in thee begin to live,
Day and night they cry to thee—
As thou art, so let us be!

2 Jesus, see my panting breast;
See, I pant in thee to rest;
Gladly would I now be clean;
Cleanse me now from every sin.

3 Fix, O fix my wav'ring mind;
To thy cross my spirit bind:
Earthly passions far remove;
Swallow up my soul in love.

4 Dust and ashes though we be,
Full of sin and misery,
Thine we are, thou son of God;
Take the purchase of thy blood.

J. WESLEY.

342

WHEN, my Saviour, shall I be
Perfectly resigned to thee?
Poor and vile in mine own eyes,
Only in thy wisdom wise?
Only thee content to know,
Ignorant of all below?
Only guided by thy light?
Only mighty in thy might?

2 So I may thy Spirit know,
   Let him as he listeth blow:
   Let the manner be unknown,
   So I may with thee be one:
   Fully in my life express
   All the heights of holiness;
   Sweetly let my spirit prove,
   All the depths of humble love.
   C. WESLEY.

MARTYN.   7th P. M.

343

JESUS, plant and root in me
  All the mind that was in thee;
Settled peace I then shall find;
Jesus' is a quiet mind.
I shall suffer and fulfil
All my Father's gracious will;
Be in all alike resign'd;
Jesus' is a patient mind.

2 When 'tis deeply rooted here,
  Perfect love shall cast out fear;
  Fear doth servile spirits bind;
  Jesus' is a noble mind.
  I shall nothing know beside
  Jesus, and him crucified:
  Perfectly to him be join'd;
  Jesus' is a loving mind.
  C. WESLEY.

CONSECRATION AND HOLINESS.

MEAR. C. M.

344

O JESUS! at thy feet we wait,
　Till thou shalt bid us rise;
Restored to our unsinning state—
　To love's sweet paradise.

2 Saviour from sin, we thee receive—
　From all indwelling sin;
Thy blood, we steadfastly believe,
　Shall make us throughly clean.

3 Since thou wouldst have us free from sin,
　And pure as those above;
Make haste to bring thy nature in,
　And perfect us in love.
C. WESLEY.

345

I KNOW that my Redeemer lives,
　And ever prays for me:
A token of his love he gives—
　A pledge of liberty.

2 He wills that I should holy be!
　What can withstand his will?
The counsel of his grace in me
　He surely shall fulfil.

3 Jesus, I hang upon thy word;
　I steadfastly believe
Thou wilt return, and claim me, Lord,
　And to thyself receive.
C. WESLEY.

CONSECRATION AND HOLINESS.

AVON. C. M.

346

NOW, even now, I yield, I yield,
    With all my sins to part;
Redeemer, speak my pardon seal'd,
    And purify my heart.

2 O Jesus, now my heart inspire
    With that pure love of thine;
Enkindle now the heavenly fire,
    To brighten and refine.

3 Now purify my faith like gold;
    The dross of sin remove;
Melt down my spirit, Lord, and mould
    Into thy perfect love.
C. WESLEY.

347

O SAVIOUR, welcome to my heart;
    Possess thy humble throne;
Bid every rival, Lord, depart,
    And reign, O Christ, alone.

2 The world and Satan I forsake;
    To thee I all resign;
My longing heart, O Saviour, take,
    And fill with love divine.

3 O may I never turn aside,
    Nor from thy bosom flee;
Let nothing here my heart divide;
    I give it all to thee.

270. CONSECRATION AND HOLINESS.

WARE. L. M.

348

O THOU exalted Son of God,
  High seated on the Father's throne!
The gifts, the purchase of thy blood,
  To us, thy waiting saints make known.

2 Come, Holy Ghost, all sacred fire!
  Come, fill thy earthly temples now:
Emptied of every base desire,
  Reign thou within, and only thou.

3 Thy sovereign right, thy gracious claim,
  To every thought and every power—
Our lives—to glorify thy name,
  We yield in this accepted hour.

4 Fill every chamber of the soul;
  Fill all our thoughts, our passions fill;
Till under thy supreme control
  Submissive rests our cheerful will.

5 'Tis done! Thou dost this moment come:
  My longing soul is all thine own;
My heart is thy abiding home;
  Henceforth I live for thee alone.

6 The altar sanctifies the gift;
  The blood insures the boon divine:
My outstretched hands to heaven I lift,
  And claim the Father's promise mine.

7 Now rise, exulting rise, my soul!
    Triumphant sing the Saviour's praise;
  His name through earth and skies extol,
    With all my powers, through all my days.
                                REV. F. BOTTOME.

WESLEY.   L. M.

349

HE wills that I should holy be:
    That holiness I long to feel;
  That full divine conformity
    To all my Saviour's righteous will.

2 See, Lord, the travail of thy soul
    Accomplish'd in the change of mine;
  And plunge me, every whit made whole,
    In all the depths of love divine.

3 On thee, O God, my soul is stay'd,
    And waits to prove thine utmost will;
  The promise by thy mercy made,
    Thou canst, thou wilt, in me fulfil.

4 No more I stagger at thy power,
    Or doubt thy truth, which cannot move:
  Hasten the long-expected hour,
    And bless me with thy perfect love.

5 Sprinkle me, Saviour, with thy blood,
    And all thy gentleness is mine;
  And plunge me in the purple flood,
    Till all I am is lost in thine.
                                C. WESLEY.

272 CONSECRATION AND HOLINESS.

St. Martin's.   C. M.

350

JESUS, my life, thyself apply;
  Thy Holy Spirit breathe:
My vile affections crucify;
  Conform me to thy death.

2 Conqu'ror of hell, and earth, and sin,
  Still with the rebel strive:
Enter my soul and work within,
  And kill and make alive.

3 More of thy life, and more I have,
  As the old Adam dies:
Bury me, Saviour, in thy grave,
  That I with thee may rise.

4 Reign in me, Lord; thy foes control,
  Who would not own thy sway;
Diffuse thine image through my soul;
  Shine to the perfect day.

5 Scatter the last remains of sin,
  And seal me thine abode;
O make me glorious all within—
  A temple built by God!
                              C. Wesley.

351

WHEN shall I see the welcome hour
  That plants my God in me?
Spirit of health, and life and power,
  And perfect liberty.

2 Love only can the conquest win,
    The strength of sin subdue :
Come, O my Saviour, cast out sin,
    And form my soul anew.
3 No longer then my heart shall mourn,
    While sanctified by grace,
I only for his glory burn,
    And always see his face.

C. WESLEY

Old Warren.   5th P. M.

352

HEAVENLY Father, I would wear
    Angel-garments, white and fair ;
Angel-vesture, undefiled,
Wilt thou give unto thy child.

2 Take the raiment soiled away,
That I wear with shame to-day ;
Give my angel robes to me,
White with heaven's own purity.

3 Take away my cloak of pride,
And the worthless rags 'twould hide ;
Clothe me in my angel dress,
Beautiful with holiness.

4 Let me wear the white robes here,
Even on earth, my Father dear,
Holding fast thy hand, and so
Through the world unspotted go.

274 CONSECRATION AND HOLINESS.

AVON. C. M.

353

COME let us use the grace divine,
  And all, with one accord,
In a perpetual cov'nant join
  Ourselves to Christ the Lord—

2 Give up ourselves, through Jesus' power,
  His Name to glorify;
And promise, in this sacred hour,
  For God to live and die.

3 The cov'nant we this moment make
  Be ever kept in mind:
We will no more our God forsake,
  Or cast his words behind.

4 We never will throw off his fear,
  Who hears our solemn vow;
And if thou art well pleased to hear,
  Come down, and meet us now.

5 To each the cov'nant blood apply,
  Which takes our sins away;
And register our names on high,
  And keep us to that day.

C. WESLEY.

354

HELP us to help each other, Lord,
  Each other's cross to bear:
Let each his friendly aid afford,
  And feel his brother's care.

CONSECRATION AND HOLINESS. 275

2 Help us to build each other up;
　Our little stock improve;
Increase our faith, confirm our hope,
　And perfect us in love.

3 Up into thee, our living Head,
　Let us in all things grow;
Till thou hast made us free indeed,
　And spotless here below.

4 Then, when the mighty work is wrought,
　Receive thy ready bride:
Give us in heaven a happy lot
　With all the sanctified.

C. WESLEY.

SICILIAN HYMN. 　　　8th P. M.

355

WELCOME, welcome, dear Redeemer,
　Welcome to this heart of mine:
Lord I make a full surrender,
　Every power and thought be thine;
　　Thine entirely,
　Through eternal ages thine.

2 Known to all to be thy mansion,
　Earth and hell will disappear,
Or in vain attempt possession,
　When they find the Lord is near:
　　Shout, O Zion!
　Shout, ye saints, the Lord is here!

276 CONSECRATION AND HOLINESS.

IVES. 9th P. M.

356

JESUS, all-atoning Lamb,
  Thine, and only thine, I am;
Take my body, spirit, soul,
Only thou possess the whole.
Thou my one thing needful be;
Let me ever cleave to thee:
Let me choose the better part;
Let me give thee all my heart.

2 Fairer than the sons of men!
Do not let me turn again—
Leave the fountain head of bliss—
Stoop to creature happiness.
Whom have I on earth below?
Thee, and only thee, I know:
Whom have I in heaven but thee?
Thou art all in all to me.

3 Thou, O love, my portion art:
Lord, thou know'st my simple heart!
Other comforts I despise;
Love, be all my paradise.
Nothing else can I require;
Love fills up my whole desire:
All thy other gifts remove,
Still thou givest me all in love.

C. WESLEY.

CONSECRATION AND HOLINESS.

WATERFORD.   12th P. M.

357

1 O MIGHT I this moment cease
   From every work of mine;
Find the perfect holiness,
   The righteousness divine!
Let me thy salvation see;
   Let me do thy perfect will;
Live in glorious liberty,
   And all thy fulness feel.

2 O cut short the work, and make
   Me now a creature new;
For thy truth and mercy's sake,
   The gracious wonder show:
Call me forth thy witness, Lord;
   Let my life declare thy power;
To thy perfect love restored,
   O let me sin no more.

3 Fain I would the truth proclaim
   That makes me free indeed;
Glorify my Saviour's name
   And all its virtues spread.
Jesus, all our wants relieves;
   Jesus, mighty to redeem,
Saves, and to the utmost saves,
   All those that come to him.

C. WESLEY.

IX.—THE TRIUMPH AND HOME IN HEAVEN.

WEBB.

358

1 O WHEN shall I see Jesus,
  And dwell with him above?
To drink the flowing fountain
  Of everlasting love?
When shall I be delivered
  From this vain world of sin,
And with my blessed Jesus
  Drink endless pleasures in?

2 Through grace I am determined
  To conquer, though I die;
And then away to Jesus
  On wings of love I'll fly.
Farewell to sin and sorrow,
  I bid you all adieu;
And you, my friends, prove faithful,
  And on your way pursue.

3 And if you meet with trials
  And troubles on your way,
Cast all your care on Jesus,
  And don't forget to pray:
Gird on the heavenly armor
  Of faith, and hope, and love;
And when your race is ended,
  You'll reign with him above.

ZION SONGSTER, 1833.

THE TRIUMPH AND HOME IN HEAVEN. 279

WE SHALL KNOW EACH OTHER THERE.

359

1 WHEN we hear the music ringing
    In the bright celestial dome,
When sweet angel-voices singing
    Gladly bid us welcome home—
To the land of ancient story,
    Where the spirit knows no care,
In that land of light and glory;
    We shall know each other there.

2 When the holy angels meet us,
    As we go to join their band,
We shall know the friends that greet us
    In the glorious spirit land ;
We shall see the same eyes shining
    On us, as in days of yore ;
We shall feel their dear arms twining
    Fondly round us as before.

3 O ye weary, sad and tossed ones,
    Droop not, faint not by the way !
Ye shall join the loved and just ones
    In the land of perfect day !
Harp-strings touched by angel-fingers
    Murmur in my raptured ear ;
Evermore their sweet song lingers:
    We shall know each other there.

280 THE TRIUMPH AND HOME IN HEAVEN.

SILOAM. C. M.

360

MY feet are weary with the march
Over the steep hill-side;
City of God! I fain would see
Thy peaceful waters glide!

2 My hands are weary toiling on
For perishable meat;
City of God, I fain would reach,
Thy glorious mercy seat.

3 Patience, poor heart, His feet were worn,
His hands were weary too;
His garments stained and travel torn,
His head wet with the dew.

4 Love thou the path thy Saviour trod,
And patient wait thy rest;
His holy city thou shalt see,
Home of the loved and blest.

ALIDA. C. M. D.

361

THERE is a land of pure delight,
Where saints immortal reign;
Infinite day excludes the light
And pleasures banish pain.

2 There everlasting spring abides,
    And never-with'ring flowers:
Death, like a narrow sea, divides
    This heavenly land from ours.

3 Sweet fields beyond the swelling flood
    Stand dress'd in living green;
So to the Jews old Canaan stood,
    While Jordan roll'd between.

4 Could we but climb where Moses stood,
    And view the landscape o'er,
Not Jordan's stream, nor death's cold flood
    Should fright us from the shore.
                             WATTS.

362

ON Jordan's stormy banks I stand,
    And cast a wishful eye
To Canaan's fair and happy land,
    Where my possessions lie.

2 No chilling winds, or pois'nous breath,
    Can reach that healthful shore;
Sickness and sorrow, pain and death,
    Are felt and fear'd no more.

3 When shall I reach that happy place,
    And be forever blest?
When shall I see my Father's face,
    And in his bosom rest?

4 Fill'd with delight, my raptured soul
    Would here no longer stay:
Though Jordan's waves around me roll,
    Fearless I'd launch away.
                             STENNETT.

282 THE TRIUMPH AND HOME IN HEAVEN.
THE GARDEN HYMN.

363

COME brethren, dear, who know the Lord,
And taste the sweetness of his word,
In Jesus' ways go on :
Our troubles and our trials here
Will only make us richer there,
When we arrive at home.

2 We feel that Heaven is now begun,
It issues from the sparkling throne—
From Jesus' throne on high :
It comes in floods we can't contain,
We drink and drink, and drink again,
And yet we still are dry.

3 But when we come to dwell above,
And all surround the throne of love,
We'll drink a full supply :
Jesus will lead his armies through,
To living fountains, where they flow,
That never will run dry.

4 'Tis there we'll reign, and shout and sing,
And make the upper regions ring,
When all the saints get home !
Come on, come on, my brethren dear,
Soon we shall meet together there,
For Jesus bids us come.

ZION SONGSTER, 1833.

THE TRIUMPH AND HOME IN HEAVEN. 283
BREMEN. 4th P. M.

364

HOW happy is the pilgrim's lot;
How free from every anxious thought,
  From worldly hope and fear!
Confined to neither court nor cell,
His soul disdains on earth to dwell,
  He only sojourns here.

2 This happiness in part is mine,
Already saved from low design,
  From every creature-love;
Blest with the scorn of finite good,
My soul is lighten'd of its load,
  And seeks the things above.

3 There is my house and portion fair;
My treasure and my heart are there,
  And my abiding home;
For me my elder brethren stay,
And angels beckon me away,
  And Jesus bids me come.

4 I come, thy servant, Lord, replies;
I come to meet thee in the skies,
  And claim my heavenly rest!
Soon will the pilgrim's journey end;
Then, O my Saviour, Brother, Friend,
  Receive me to thy breast.

J. WESLEY.

284. THE TRIUMPH AND HOME IN HEAVEN.

ALIDA.   C. M. D.

365

SWEET rivers of redeeming love
  Lie just before mine eye;
Had I the pinions of a dove,
  I'd to those rivers fly:
I'd rise superior to my pain,
  With joy outstrip the wind;
I'd cross o'er Jordan's stormy waves,
  And leave the world behind.

2 A few more days or years at most,
  My troubles will be o'er;
I hope to join the heavenly host,
  On Canaan's happy shore.
My raptured soul shall drink and feast,
  In love's unbounded sea;
The glorious hope of endless rest.
  Is ravishing to me.

3 O come, my Saviour, come away,
  And bear me to the skies!
Nor let thy chariot wheels delay—
  Make haste and bring it nigh:
I long to see thy glorious face,
  And in thy image shine—
To triumph in victorious grace,
  And be forever thine.

ZION SONGSTER, 1833.

HAPPY LAND.

366

THERE is a happy land,
   Far, far, away,
Where saints in glory stand
   Bright, bright as day:
O how they sweetly sing—
Worthy is our Saviour King;
Loud let his praises ring,
   Forever more.

2 Come to this happy land,
   Come, come away;
Why will ye doubting stand?
   Why still delay?
O we shall happy be,
When from sin and sorrow free,
Lord, we shall live with thee,
   Blest evermore.

3 Bright in that happy land
   Beams every eye,
Kept by a Father's hand,
   Love cannot die.
O, then, to glory run;
Be a crown and kingdom own;
And bright above the sun,
   Reign evermore.

286 THE TRIUMPH AND HOME IN HEAVEN.
REST FOR THE WEARY.

367

IN the Christian's home in glory,
There remains a land of rest;
There my Saviour's gone before me,
To fulfil my soul's request.

    There is rest for the weary,
    There is rest for the weary,
    There is rest for the weary,
    There is rest for you;
    On the other side of Jordan,
    In the sweet fields of Eden,
    Where the tree of life is blooming,
    There is rest for you.

2 He is fitting up my mansion,
Which eternally shall stand;
For my stay shall not be transient,
In that holy, happy land.

3 Pain nor sickness ne'er shall enter,
Grief nor woe, my lot shall share,
But in that celestial centre,
I a crown of life shall wear.

4 Death itself shall then be vanquished,
And his sting shall be withdrawn;
Shout for gladness, O, ye ransomed!
Hail with joy the rising morn.

THE TRIUMPH AND HOME IN HEAVEN. 287

5 Sing, O sing, ye heirs of glory,
  Shout your triumph as you go;
  Zion's gates will open for you,
  You shall find an entrance through.

REV. W. McDONALD.

OLD TUNE.   SACRED MELODIES, p. 40.

368

THERE is a Heaven above the skies—
  A Heaven where pleasure never dies—
A Heaven I sometimes hope to see,
Yet often fear 'tis not for me.

2 The way is difficult and straight,
  And narrow is the Gospel gate;
  Ten thousand dangers are therein—
  Ten thousand snares to take me in.

3 Through glimm'ring hopes and gloomy fears,
  Dimly the heavenly way appears;
  But in this way I clearly see
  The track of him who died for me.

4 Then, O my soul arise and sing!
  Behold thy Saviour, Friend, and King!
  With pleasing smiles he now looks down,
  And cries—"Press on and take the crown."

5 "Prove faithful, then, a few more days;
  Fight the good fight and win the race;
  And then thy soul with me shall reign,
  Thy head a crown of glory gain."

ZION SONGSTER, 1833

288. THE TRIUMPH AND HOME IN HEAVEN.
DE FLEURY.

369

AWAY with our sorrow and fear,
   We soon shall recover our home;
The city of saints shall appear—
   The day of eternity come.
From earth we shall quickly remove,
   And mount to our native abode—
The house of our Father above—
   The palace of angels and God.

2 Our mourning is all at an end,
   When, raised by the life-giving Word,
We see the new city descend,
   Adorn'd as a bride for her Lord:
The city so holy and clean,
   No sorrow can breathe in the air:
No gloom of affliction or sin;
   No shadow of evil is there.

3 By faith we already behold
   That lovely Jerusalem here:
Her walls are of jasper and gold;
   As crystal her buildings are clear;
Immovably founded in grace,
   She stands as she ever hath stood,
And brightly her Builder displays,
   And flames with the glory of God.
C. WESLEY.

THE TRIUMPH AND HOME IN HEAVEN.

LOOKING HOME.

From Golden Shower, by permission of W. B. BRADBURY.

370

AH, this heart is void and chill,
   'Mid earth's noisy thronging;
For my Father's mansions still
   Earnestly is longing.

CHORUS.

      Looking home, looking home,
      Towards the heavenly mansions
      Jesus hath prepared for me,
      In his Father's kingdom

2 Soon the glorious day will dawn,
   Heavenly pleasure bringing;
Night will be exchanged for morn,
   Sighs give place to singing.

3 Oh! to be at home again,
   All for which we're sighing,
From all earthly want and pain
   To be swiftly flying.

4 Blessed home, oh! blessed home,
   All for which we're sighing;
Soon our Lord will bid us come
   To our Father's kingdom.

290. THE TRIUMPH AND HOME IN HEAVEN.
Beautiful City.

371

1. BEAUTIFUL Zion, built above,
Beautiful city, that I love,
Beautiful gates of pearly white,
Beautiful temple—God its light!
He who was slain on Calvary
Opens those pearly gates to me.

2 Beautiful heaven, where all is light,
Beautiful angels, clothed in white,
Beautiful strains, that never tire,
Beautiful harps through all the choir!
There shall I join the chorus sweet,
Worshipping at the Saviour's feet.

3 Beautiful crowns on every brow,
Beautiful palms the conquerors show,
Beautiful robes the ransomed wear,
Beautiful all who enter there!
Thither I press with eager feet;
There shall my rest be long and sweet.

4 Beautiful throne for Christ our King,
Beautiful songs the angels sing,
Beautiful rest, all wanderings cease,
Beautiful home of perfect peace!
There shall my eye the Saviour see:
Haste to this heavenly home with me.

THE TRIUMPH AND HOME IN HEAVEN. 291

LILLY DALE.

372

JERUSALEM, my happy home.
　Name ever dear to me,
When shall my labors have an end,
　In joy and peace in thee?

CHORUS.
O Heaven, sweet Heaven, home of the blest!
　How I long to be there,
In its glories to share,
　And to lean on Jesus' breast.

2 Why should I shrink at pain or wo,
　Or feel at death dismay?
I've Canaan's goodly land in view,
　And realms of endless day.

3 Jerusalem, my happy home,
　My soul still pants for thee;
Then shall my labors have an end
　When I thy joys shall see.　ZION SONGSTER.

LAND OF REST.

373

O LAND of rest! for thee I sigh;
　When will the moment come,
When I shall lay my armor by,
　And dwell with Christ at home?

2 No tranquil joys on earth I know;
　No peaceful, sheltering dome;
This world's a wilderness of wo,
　This world is not my home.

3 To Jesus Christ I sought for rest,
　He bade me cease to roam,
And fly for succor to his breast,
　And he'd conduct me home.

4 Weary of wandering round and round
　This vale of sin and gloom,
I long to leave th' unhallowed ground
　And dwell with Christ at home.
SAC. MELODIES.

374

COME, let us join our friends above,
　That have obtain'd the prize;
And on the eagle wings of love
　To joys celestial rise.

2 One family we dwell in Him,
　One church above, beneath,
Though now divided by the stream,
　The narrow stream of death.

3 One army of the living God,
　To his command we bow;
Part of his host have cross'd the flood,
　And part are crossing now.

4 His militant embodied host,
　With wishful looks we stand,
And long to see that happy coast,
　And reach the heavenly land.
C. WESLEY.

THE TRIUMPH AND HOME IN HEAVEN.

Going Home.

375

WE go the way that leads to God,
  The way that saints have ever trod;
So let us leave this sinful shore,
For realms where we shall die no more.

CHORUS.

  We're going home, we're going home,
  We're going home, to die no more;
  To die no more, to die no more,
  We're going home to die no more.

2 The ways of God are ways of bliss,
  And all his paths are happiness;
  Then, weary souls, your sighs give o'er,
  We're going home to die no more.

3 There is a land, beyond the sky,
  Where happy spirits never sigh;
  Then, erring souls, your sins deplore,
  And go to heaven to die no more.

4 Come, sinners come, O come along,
  And join our happy pilgrim throng;
  Farewell, vain world, and all your store;
  We're going home to die no more.

5 Come let us tread the sacred road
  That holy saints and martyrs trod;
  Wage to the end the glorious strife,
  And win, like them, a crown of life.

SAC. MEL.

294 THE TRIUMPH AND HOME IN HEAVEN.

A BEAUTIFUL LAND.   GOLD CHAIN.

376

A BEAUTIFUL land by faith I see,
  A land of rest, from sorrow free;
The home of the ransomed bright and fair;
  And beautiful angels too are there.

CHORUS.

    Will you go? Will you go?
    Go to that beautiful land with me?
    Will you go? Will you go?
    Go to that beautiful land?

2 That beautiful land, the city of light,
  It ne'er has known the shades of night;
The glory of God, the light of day,
  Hath driven the darkness far away.

3 The heavenly throng arrayed in white,
  In rapture range the plains of light;
And in one harmonious choir they raise
  Their glorious Savior's matchless grace.

377

MY heavenly home is bright and fair;
  We'll be gathered home;
Nor death, nor sighing, visit there,
  We'll be gathered home.

We'll wait till Jesus comes,
We'll wait till Jesus comes,
We'll wait till Jesus comes,
And we'll be gathered home.

2 Its glittering towers the sun outshine,
That heavenly mansion shall be mine.

3 My Father's house is built on high,
Above the bright and starry sky.

4 When from this earthly prison free,
That heavenly mansion mine shall be.

GREENWOOD. 7th P. M.

378

PALMS of glory, raiment white,
  Crowns that never fade away,
Gird and deck the saints in light,
  Priests and kings and conquerors they;
Yet the conquerors bring their palms
  To the Lamb amidst the throne,
And proclaim in joyful psalms,
  Victory through his cross alone.

2 Kings, for harps their crowns resign,
  Crying, as they strike the chords:
"Take the kingdom! it is thine,
  King of kings and Lord of lords."
Round the altar, priests confess,
  If their robes are white as snow,
'Twas the Savior's righteousness
  And his blood that made them so.

296 THE TRIUMPH AND HOME IN HEAVEN.
No Sorrow There.

379

COME sing to me of Heaven
  When I'm about to die,
Sing songs of holy ecstacy
  To waft my soul on high.

CHORUS.

There'll be no sorrow there,
There'll be no sorrow there,
In Heaven above, where all is love,
There'll be no sorrow there.

2 When cold and sluggish drops
    Roll off my marble brow,
  Break forth in songs of joyfulness;
    Let Heaven begin below.

3 When the last moments come,
    O, watch my dying face,
  To catch the bright seraphic glow
    Which in each feature plays.

4 Then to my raptured ear
    Let one sweet song be given;
  Let music charm me last on earth,
    And greet me first in Heaven.

5 Then close my sightless eyes,
    And lay me down to rest,
  And clasp my cold and icy hands,
    Upon my lifeless breast.

6 When round my senseless clay
    Assemble those I love,
Then sing of heaven, delightful heaven,
    My glorious home above.

THE HAPPY HOME.
From Golden Chain, by permission of W. B. BRADBURY.

380

I AM bound for the land of the living;
    O hinder me not on my way:
The sunlight is brightening before me,
    That heralds eternity's day.
The flowers that bloom in my pathway,
    Breathe odors that waft me right on;
They lure me no longer to tarry,
    But welcome earth's time to be gone.

REFRAIN.

2 There's a happy home beyond this world of
A home above, where all is love,   [care,
And the good shall all meet there.

2 I am weaned from this land of the dying;
    Decay is enstamped everywhere;
Earth's pleasures are seeming and fleeting;
    My soul has grown weak with its care.
The joy-rays of life are remembered
    Like sleep-thoughts that float through the
The flesh and the spirit are warring, [brain;
    Each striving the mastery to gain.

3 I am waiting the summons that bids me
   No longer a pilgrim to roam,
But, leaving the past in this death-land,
   Make the land of the living my home.
The messenger-angel stands waiting
   The signal to whisper to me,
That the place is prepared for my dwelling,
   And the Master is calling for me.

MY FATHER LAND. 9s & 8s.

381

THERE is a place where my hopes are stayed;
   My heart and my treasure are there;
Where verdure and blossoms never fade,
   And fields are forever fair.

CHORUS.
   That blissful place is my Fatherland;
      By faith its delight I explore:
   Come favor my flight, angelic band,
      And waft me in peace to that shore.

2 There is a place where the angels dwell —
   A pure and a peaceful abode;
The joys of that place no tongue can tell;
   But there is the palace of God.

3 There is a place where my friends are gone,
   Who suffered and worshipped with me:
Exalted with Christ upon his throne,
   The King in his beauty they see.

4 There is a place where I hope to live,
   When life and its labors are o'er—
A place which the Lord to me will give;
   And then I shall sorrow no more.
                        REV. W. HUNTER.

THE TRIUMPH AND HOME IN HEAVEN. 299
DENNIS. S. M.

382
ONE sweetly solemn thought
    Comes to me o'er and o'er—
I'm nearer to my home to-day
    Than I have been before;

2 Nearer my Father's house,
    Where many mansions be—
Yet nearer to the great white throne,
    And near the jasper sea;

3 Nearer the bound of life,
    Where we lay burdens down;
Yet nearer laying down the cross
    And nearer to the crown.

4 But, lying dark between,
    And winding through the night,
There is a dim and unknown stream
    Whose farther shore is bright.

5 O Saviour take my hand!
    O help my feeble faith!
Give me to feel as when I stand
    Upon the shore of death!

6 To feel as when my feet
    Are slipping o'er the brink!
For NOW I may be nearer it—
    Much nearer than I think!

300 THE TRIUMPH AND HOME IN HEAVEN.
SHINING SHORE,

From S. S. Bell, by permission G. F. ROOT.

383

MY days are gliding swiftly by,
   And I, a pilgrim stranger,
Would not detain them as they fly,—
   Those hours of toil and danger.

CHORUS.
   For O, we stand on Jordan's strand;
     Our friends are passing over;
   And just before, the shining shore
     We may almost discover.

2 We'll gird our loins, my brethren dear,
   Our distant home discerning;
  Our absent Lord has left us word—
   Let every lamp be burning.

3 Should coming days be cold and dark,
   We need not cease our singing:
  That perfect rest naught can molest,
   Where golden harps are ringing.

4 Let sorrow's rudest tempest blow,
   Each chord on earth to sever,
  Our King says come, and there's our home,
   Forever! O, forever!

   LET ME GO.

384

LET me go where saints are going,
  To the mansions of the blest;
Let me go where my Redeemer
  Has prepared his people's rest.
I would gain the realms of brightness,
  Where they dwell for evermore;
I would join the friends that wait me,
  Over on the other shore.
    Let me go; 'tis Jesus calls me;
      Let me gain the realms of day;
    Bear me over, angel pinions;
      Longs my soul to be away.

2 Let me go where none are weary—
  Where is raised no wail of woe;
Let me go and bathe my spirit,
  In the raptures angels know.
Let me go, for bliss eternal,
  Lures my soul away, away,
And the victor's song triumphant,
  Thrills my heart; I cannot stay.

3 Let me go; why should I tarry?
  What has earth to bind me here?
What but cares and toils and sorrows?
  What but death and pain and fear?
Let me go, for hopes most cherished,
  Blasted round me often lie.
O! I've gathered brightest flowers,
  But to see them fade and die.

REV. L. HARTSOUGH.

302. THE TRIUMPH AND HOME IN HEAVEN.
HEAVEN IS MY HOME.

385

I'M but a stranger here;
  Heaven is my home.
Earth is a desert drear;
  Heaven is my home.
  Dangers and sorrows stand
  Round me on every hand;
  Heaven is my Father-land;
  Heaven is my home.

2 What though the tempests rage,
  Heaven is my home.
Short is my pilgrimage;
  Heaven is my home.
  Time's cold and wintry blast
  Soon will be overpast;
  I shall reach home at last:
  Heaven is my home

3 There at my Saviour's side;
  Heaven is my home.
I shall be glorified;
  Heaven is my home.
  There are the good and blest,
  Those I love most and best;
  There, too, I soon shall rest;
  Heaven is my home.

THE TRIUMPH AND HOME IN HEAVEN. 303
De Fleury.

386

I LONG to behold Him array'd
    With glory and light from above;
The King in his beauty display'd,—
    His beauty of holiest love;
I languish and sigh to be there,
    Where Jesus hath fix'd his abode;
O when shall we meet in the air,
    And fly to the mountain of God?

2 With him I on Zion shall stand,
    For Jesus hath spoken the word;
The breadth of Immanuel's land
    Survey by the light of my Lord:
But when, on thy bosom reclined,
    Thy face I am strengthen'd to see,
My fulness of rapture I find,—
    My heaven of heavens in thee.

3 The saints in his presence receive
    Their great and eternal reward;
In Jesus, in heaven, they live,—
    They reign in the smile of their Lord.
The flame of angelical love
    Is kindled at Jesus's face;
And all the enjoyment above,
    Consists in the rapturous gaze.

C. Wesley.

304 THE TRIUMPH AND HOME IN HEAVEN.
PACKARD. C. M. D.

387

O CHRISTIANS! are you ready now
To cross the swelling flood?
On Canaan's happy shore behold,
And see your smiling God!
The dazzling charms of that bright world
Attract my soul above:
My tongue shall shout redeeming grace,
When perfected in love.

2 Go on, my brethren in the Lord;
I'm bound to meet you there:
Although you tread enchanted ground,
Be bold and never fear.
Fight on, fight on, ye valiant souls;
Your Captain is in view,
And when you gain fair Canaan's shore,
I hope to meet with you.

3 Salvation! through our conquering king!
Now let the echo fly;
While they repeat the song above,
Through armies in the sky.
O, Christians! help me praise the Lamb
Who died for you and me!
We'll sing his praises as we go,
And shout eternally.

THE TRIUMPH AND HOME IN HEAVEN. 305

WHITE ROBES.

388

LIFT your eyes of faith, and see
Saints with angels join'd in one!
What a countless company
Stand before yon dazzling throne!

CHORUS.
They have clean robes, white robes;
White robes are waiting for me;
Yes, clean robes, white robes,
Washed in the blood of the Lamb.

2 Each before his Saviour stands,
All in whitest robes array'd;
Palms they carry in their hands,
Crowns of glory on their head.

3 These are they that bore the cross;
Nobly for their Master stood;
Suff'rers in his righteous cause;
Foll'wers of the dying God.

4 Out of great distress they came;
Wash'd their robes, by faith, below,
In the blood of yonder Lamb—
Blood that washes white as snow;

5 Therefore are they next the throne;
Serve their Maker day and night:
God resides among his own,
God doth in his saints delight.

C. WESLEY.

306. THE TRIUMPH AND HOME IN HEAVEN.
SWEET REST.

389

COME, brethren, don't grow weary,
   But let us journey on;
The moments will not tarry,
   This life will soon be gone.
The passing scenes all tell us,
   That death will surely come:
These bodies soon will molder
   In the dark and weary tomb.

CHORUS.
   There is sweet rest in Heaven,
   There is sweet rest in Heaven,
   There is sweet rest, there is sweet rest,
   There is sweet rest in Heaven.

2 Loved ones have gone before us,
   They beckon us away;
O'er heavenly plains they're soaring,
   Blest in eternal day:
But we are in the army,
   And dare not leave our post;
We'll fight until we conquer
   The foe's most mighty host.

WILLOUGHBY.   SINGING PILGRIM p. 75.

390

1. Come on, my partners in distress,
My comrades through the wilderness,
  Who still your bodies feel:
Awhile forget your griefs and fears,
And look beyond this vale of tears,
  To that celestial hill.

2 Beyond the bounds of time and space,
Look forward to that heavenly place,
  The saints' secure abode;
On faith's strong eagle pinions rise,
And force your passage to the skies,
  And scale the mount of God.

3 Who suffer with our Master here,
We shall before his face appear,
  And by his side sit down;
To patient faith the prize is sure;
And all that to the end endure
  The cross, shall wear the crown.

4 Thrice blessed, bliss-inspiring hope!
It lifts the fainting spirits up;
  It brings to life the dead:
Our conflicts here shall soon be past,
And you and I ascend at last,
  Triumphant with our Head.

5 That great mysterious Deity,
We soon with open face shall see;
  The beatific sight
Shall fill the heavenly courts with praise,
And wide diffuse the golden blaze
  Of everlasting light.

C. WESLEY.

308 THE TRIUMPH AND HOME IN HEAVEN.
BOWER OF PRAYER.

391

I WOULD not live alway; I ask not to stay
Where storm after storm rises dark o'er the way;
The few lurid mornings that dawn on us here
Are enough for life's joys, full enough for its cheer.

2 I would not live alway; no—welcome the tomb!
Since Jesus hath lain there, I dread not its gloom!
There sweet be my rest till he bid me arise,
To hail him in triumph descending the skies.

3 Who, who would live alway, away from his God—
Away from yon heaven, that blissful abode,
Where rivers of pleasure flow bright o'er the plains,
And the noontide of glory eternally reigns?

4 There saints of all ages in harmony meet,
Their Saviour and brethren transported to greet,
While anthems of rapture unceasingly roll,
And the smile of the Lord is the feast of the soul.
MUHLENBURG.

BONNY DOON.   L. M. D.

392

LO! round the throne a glorious band,
The saints in countless myriads stand;
Of every tongue redeem'd to God,
Array'd in garments wash'd in blood.

2 Through tribulation great they came;
  They bore the cross, despised the shame;
  But now from all their labors rest,
  In God's eternal glory blest.

3 They see the Saviour face to face;
  They sing the triumph of his grace;
  And day and night, with ceaseless praise,
  To him their loud hosannas raise.

4 O, may we tread the sacred road
  That holy saints and martyrs trod;
  Wage to the end the glorious strife,
  And win, like them, a crown of life.

A HOME IN HEAVEN.   GOLDEN CHAIN.

393

A HOME in Heaven! What a joyful thought,
  As the poor man toils in his weary lot!
His heart oppressed, and with anguish driven,
From his home below to his home in Heaven.

2 A home in Heaven! when our friends are fled,
  To the cheerless gloom of the moldering dead;
  We wait in hope on the promise given;
  We will meet up there, in our home in Heaven.

3 A home in Heaven! when the wheel is broke,
  And the golden bowl by the terror-stroke;
  When life's bright sun sinks in deaths dark even,
  We will then ascend to our home in Heaven.
                              REV. W. HUNTER.

310 THE TRIUMPH AND HOME IN HEAVEN.
My Immortal Home.

394

My latest sun is sinking fast,
  My race is nearly run;
My strongest trials now are past,
  My triumph is begun.

CHORUS.

  O come, angel band,
  Come and around me stand;
  O bear me away on your snowy wings,
  To my immortal home.

2 I know I'm nearing the holy ranks,
    Of friends and kindred dear,
  For I brush the dews on Jordan's banks;
    The crossing must be near.

3 I have almost gained my heavenly home,
    My spirit loudly sings;
  The holy ones, behold, they come!
    I hear the noise of wings.

4 O, bear my longing heart to Him
    Who bled and died for me;
  Whose blood now cleanses from all sin,
    And gives me victory.

REV. J. HASKELL.

THE TRIUMPH AND HOME IN HEAVEN. 311
Forever with the Lord. S. M. D.

395

FOREVER with the Lord!
  Amen, so let it be!
Life from the dead is in that word,
  'Tis immortality.
2 Here in the body pent,
    Absent from Him I roam;
  Yet nightly pitch my moving tent
    A day's march nearer home.
3 Forever with the Lord!
    Father, if 'tis thy will,
  The promise of that faithful word,
    E'en here to me fulfil.
4 So, when my latest breath
    Shall rend the veil in twain,
  By death I shall escape from death,
    And life eternal gain.

396

WE know, by faith we know,
  If this vile house of clay,
This tabernacle, sink below,
  In ruinous decay,
2 We have a house above,
    Not made with mortal hands;
  And firm as our Redeemer's love
    That heavenly fabric stands.

C. WESLEY

312. THE TRIUMPH AND HOME IN HEAVEN.
BRATTLE STREET..

397

AND let this feeble body fail,
  And let it faint or die;
My soul shall quit the mournful vale,
  And soar to worlds on high:
Shall join the disembodied saints,
  And find its long-sought rest,—
That only bliss for which it pants.
  In the Redeemer's breast.

2 In hope of that immortal crown
    I now the cross sustain,
  And gladly wander up and down,
    And smile at toil and pain:
  I suffer on my threescore years,
    Till my Deliv'rer come,
  And wipe away his servant's tears,
    And take his exile home.

3 O what hath Jesus bought for me!
    Before my ravish'd eyes
  Rivers of life divine I see,
    And trees of Paradise:
  I see a world of spirits bright,
    Who taste the pleasures there:
  They all are robed in spotless white,
    And conqu'ring palms they bear.

C. WESLEY.

THE TRIUMPH AND HOME IN HEAVEN.

FOREVER WITH THE LORD.   S. M.

398

THERE is no night in heaven;
  In that blest world above,
Work never can bring weariness,
  For work itself is love.
There is no grief in heaven;
  For life is one glad day,
And tears are of those former things
  Which all have passed away.

2 There is no want in heaven;
    The Lamb of God supplies
  Life's tree of twelvefold fruitage still,
    Life's spring which never dries.
  There is no sin in heaven;
    Behold that blessed throng;
  All holy is their spotless robe,
    All holy is their song.

3 There is no death in heaven;
    For they who gain that shore
  Have won their immortality,
    And they can die no more.
  There is no death in heaven;
    But when the Christian dies,
  Angels await his parted soul,
    And waft it to the skies!

314 THE TRIUMPH AND HOME IN HEAVEN.
WORLD OF LIGHT.

399

1. THERE is a beautiful world,
   Where saints and angels sing,
A world where peace and pleasure reigns,
   And heavenly praises ring.

CHORUS.
   We'll be there, we'll be there,
Palms of victory, crowns of glory we shall
   In that beautiful world on high. [wear

2 There is a beautiful world,
   Where sorrow never comes;
A world where tears shall never fall,
   In sorrow for our home.

3 There is a beautiful world,
   Unseen to mortal sight;
And darkness never enters there:
   That home is fair and bright.

4 There is a beautiful world,
   Of harmony and love;
O, may we safely enter there,
   And dwell with God above.

I'M A LONELY TRAVELLER. Sac. Mel.

THE TRIUMPH AND HOME IN HEAVEN. 315

400
I'M a lonely traveller here,
  Weary, oppressed;
But my journey's end is near;
  Soon I shall rest.
Dark and dreary is the way
  Toiling I've come;
Ask me not with you to stay,
  Yonder's my home.

2 I'm a traveller to a land
  Where all is fair;
Where is seen no broken band;
  All, all, are there.
Where no tear shall ever fall
  Nor heart be sad;
Where the glory is for all,
  And all are glad.

3 I'm a traveller, and I go
  Where all is fair;
Farewell all I've loved below,
  I must be there;
Worldly honors, hopes and gains,
  All, I resign;
Welcome sorrow, grief and pain,
  If Heaven be mine.

4 I'm a traveller, call me not;
  Upward's my way;
Yonder is my rest and lot;
  I cannot stay.
Farewell earthly pleasures all;
  Pilgrim I'll roam;
Hail me not! In vain you call,
  Yonder's my home.

316 THE TRIUMPH AND HOME IN HEAVEN.
ALIDA.   C. M. D.

401

1. HOW happy every child of grace,
Who knows his sins forgiven!
This earth, he cries, is not my place;
I seek my place in heaven:
A country far from mortal sight,
Yet, O, by faith I see;
The land of rest, the saints' delight—
The heaven prepared for me.

2 O what a blessed hope is ours!
While here on earth we stay,
We more than taste the heavenly powers,
And ante-date the day:
We feel the resurrection near,—
Our life in Christ concealed,—
And with his glorious presence here
Our earthen vessels fill'd.

3 O would he more of heaven bestow!
And when the vessels break,
Let our triumphant spirits go
To grasp the God we seek;
In rapturous awe on him to gaze,
Who bought the sight for me;
And shout and wonder at his grace
To all eternity.

                                C. WESLEY.

THE TRIUMPH AND HOME IN HEAVEN. 317
De Fleury.

402

O WHEN shall we sweetly remove;
   O when shall we enter our rest,—
Return to the Zion above,
   The mother of spirits distress'd;
The city of God the great King,
   Where sorrow and death are no more,
Where saints our Immanuel sing,
   And cherub and seraph adore?

2 But angels themselves cannot tell
   The joys of that holiest place,
Where Jesus is pleased to reveal
   The light of his heavenly face:
When, caught in the rapturous flame,
   The sight beatific they prove;
And walk in the light of the Lamb,
   Enjoying the beams of his love.

3 Thou know'st in the spirit of prayer
   We long thy appearing to see,
Resign'd to the burden we bear,
   But longing to triumph with thee:
'Tis good at thy word to be here;
   'Tis better in thee to be gone,
And see thee in glory appear,
   And rise to a share in thy throne.

C. Wesley.

318 THE TRIUMPH AND HOME IN HEAVEN.
WARWICK. C. M.

403

GIVE me the wings of faith to rise
  Within the veil, and see
The saints above how great their joys,
  How bright their glories be.

2 Once they were mourners here below,
  And poured out cries and tears;
They wrestled hard, as we do now,
  With sins, and doubts, and fears.

3 I ask them whence their vic'try came:
  They, with united breath,
Ascribe their conquest to the Lamb,—
  Their triumph to his death.

4 They mark'd the footsteps that he trod;
  His zeal inspired their breast;
And, following their incarnate God,
  Possess the promised rest.
                              WATTS.

404

HAPPY the souls to Jesus join'd,
  And saved by grace alone;
Walking in all his ways, they find
  Their heaven on earth begun.

2 The church triumphant in thy love,
  Their mighty joys we know:
They sing the Lamb in hymns above,
  And we in hymns below.

THE TRIUMPH AND HOME IN HEAVEN. 319

3 Thee in thy glorious realm they praise,
    And bow before thy throne;
We in the kingdom of thy grace:
    The kingdoms are but one.
4 The holy to the holiest leads,
    And thence our spirits rise;
For he that in thy statutes treads,
    Shall meet thee in the skies.

C. WESLEY.

HARWELL.   9th P. M.

405
THIS is not my place of resting,
    Mine's a city yet to come;
Onward to it I am hasting—
    On to my eternal home.
2 In it all is light and glory,
    O'er it shines an endless day;
Every trace of sin's sad story,
    All the curse has passed away.
3 There the Lamb—our Shepherd, leads us,
    By the streams of life along;
On the freshest pastures feeds us,
    Turns our sighing into song.
4 Soon we pass this desert dreary
    Soon we bid farewell to pain;
Never more be sad or weary,
    Never, never sin again.

BONAR.

X.—CLOSING HYMNS & DOXOLOGIES.

No Parting There.

406

HERE we meet to part again,
Here we meet to part again;
But when we meet on Canaan's plain
There'll be no parting there.
    In that bright world above;
    Shout! shout the victory!
    We're on our journey home.

2 Here we meet to part again,
But when a seat in Heaven we gain,
There'll be no parting there.

3 Here we meet to part again,
But there we shall with Jesus reign,
There'll be no parting there.

SACRED MELODIES.

DENNIS.   S. M.

407

BLEST be the tie that binds
Our hearts in Christian love;
The fellowship of kindred minds
  Is like to that above.

CLOSING HYMNS AND DOXOLOGIES. 321

2 Before our Father's throne,
  We pour our ardent prayers;
Our fears, our hopes, our aims are one—
  Our comforts and our cares.

3 We share our mutual woes;
  Our mutual burdens bear;
And often for each other flows
  The sympathizing tear.

4 When we asunder part,
  It gives us inward pain;
But we shall still be join'd in heart,
  And hope to meet again.

5 This glorious hope revives
  Our courage by the way;
While each in expectation lives,
  And longs to see the day.

FAWCETT.

OLD WARREN.   5th P. M.

408

CHRISTIAN brethren, ere we part,
  Every voice and every heart
Join, and to our Father raise
One last hymn of grateful praise.

2 Though we here should meet no more,
Yet there is a brighter shore;
Where, released from toil and pain,
We all, through grace, shall meet again.

CLOSING HYMNS AND DOXOLOGIES.

O THAT WILL BE JOYFUL.

409

TOGETHER let us sweetly live;
  Together let us die;
And each a starry crown receive,
  And reign above the sky.

CHORUS.
      O that will be joyful, joyful, joyful,
        O that will be joyful
      To meet to part no more:
      To meet to part no more,
      On Canaan's happy shore;
      There we shall meet at Jesus' feet—
        Shall meet to part no more

2 And if our fellowship below
    In Jesus be so sweet,
  What height of rapture shall we know
    When round his throne we meet!

3 When we've been there ten thousand years,
    Bright shining as the sun,
  We've no less days to sing God's praise
    Than when we first begun.

DOXOLOGY.

410

TO Father, Son, and Holy Ghost,
  Who sweetly all agree
To save a world of sinners lost,
  Eternal glory be.

WATTS.

CLOSING HYMNS AND DOXOLOGIES. 323

CARMARTHEN. 3d P. M.

411

JESUS, accept the praise
   That to thy Name belongs;
Matter of all our lays,
   Subject of all our songs:
Through thee we now together came,
And part exulting in thy Name.

2 O let us thus go on
   In all thy pleasant ways,
And, armed with patience, run
   With joy the' appointed race:
Keep us and every seeking soul,
Till all attain the heavenly goal.

3 There we shall meet again,
   When all our toils are o'er,
And death, and grief, and pain,
   And parting are no more:
We shall with all our brethren rise,
And hail thee in the flaming skies.

4 O happy, happy day,
   That calls thy exiles home;
The heavens shall pass away,
   The earth receive its doom:
Earth we shall view, and heaven, destroy'd,
And shout above the fiery void.

C. WESLEY.

324 CLOSING HYMNS AND DOXOLOGIES.
Sicilian.

412

LORD, dismiss us with thy blessing,
　Fill our hearts with joy and peace;
Let us each, thy love possessing,
　Triumph in redeeming grace.
　　O refresh us,
Travelling through this wilderness.

2 Thanks we give and adoration
　For thy Gospel's joyful sound;
May the fruits of thy salvation
　In our hearts and lives abound.
　　May thy presence
With us evermore be found.

3 So whene'er the signal's given
　Us from earth to call away,
Borne on angel's wings to Heaven,
　Called the summons to obey,
　　May we ever
Reign with thee in endless day.

DOXOLOGY.　　　　　　　　　　L. M.

413

PRAISE God, from whom all blessings flow;
　Praise him, all creatures here below;
Praise him above, ye heavenly host;
Praise Father, Son, and Holy Ghost.

INDEX.

	PAGE.
Abba, Father, hear thy child	109
A beautiful land by faith I see	294
A charge to keep I have	189
A fountain in Jesus which runs always free	66
A fountain of life and of grace	127
A home in Heaven, what a joyful thought	309
Ah! this heart is void and chill	289
Ah! whither should I go	86
Alas! and did my Saviour bleed	115
Almighty God, thy piercing eye	37
All glory and praise to Jesus our Lord	162
All hail the power of Jesus' name	163
All praise to the Lamb, accepted I am	162
All that I was, my sin, my guilt	219
Amazing sight! the Saviour stands	59
Am I a soldier of the cross	222
And am I born to die	31
And am I only born to die	30
And can I yet delay	103
And can it be that I should gain	104
And can'st thou sinner, slight	28
And let this feeble body fail	312
And must I be to judgment brought	43
Arise and bless the Lord	146
Arise, my soul arise	118
Arise my soul on wings sublime	183
Author of faith, Eternal Word	120
Awake and sing the song	179
Awake my soul in joyful lays	136
Awake my soul, stretch every nerve	224
Awaked by Sinai's awful sound	153

Away my unbelieving fear.................................. 190
Away with our sorrow and fear........................... 288
Beautiful Zion, built above................................. 290
Because for me the Saviour prays........................ 76
Before thy throne we bow.................................. 18
Begone unbelief! my Saviour is near..................... 215
Behold a Stranger at the door............................. 46
Behold, behold the Lamb of God......................... 122
Behold, I come with joy to do............................. 205
Being of beings, God of love............................... 254
Be it my only wisdom here................................. 192
Beneath our feet and o'er our head....................... 38
Blest be our Everlasting Lord.............................. 168
Blest be the tie that binds.................................. 320
Blow ye the trumpet, blow................................. 56
Broad is the road that leads to death.................... 32
By faith I to the fountain fly.............................. 108
By faith I view my Saviour dying......................... 126
By thy birth and by thy tears............................. 87
Call'd from above I rise.................................... 245
Children of the Heavenly King............................ 221
Christian brethren ere we part............................ 321
Christian, the morn breaks sweetly o'er thee 212
Christians, I am on my journey........................... 193
Come brethren dear who know the Lord............... 282
Come brethren don't grow weary......................... 306
Come Holy Ghost, all-quickening fire 240
Come, Holy Ghost, inspire our songs.................... 7
Come humble sinner, in whose breast.................... 58
Come let us all unite and sing............................ 175
Come let us join our cheerful songs...................... 158
Come let us join our friends above....................... 292
Come let us sing of Jesus.................................. 138
Come let us tune our loftiest songs...................... 137

Come let us use the grace divine	274
Come, my brethren, let us try	197
Come, my soul, thy suit prepare	8
Come, O my soul, in sacred lays	136
Come, O thou greater than my heart	250
Come, O ye sinners, to the Lord	68
Come on my partners in distress	307
Come Saviour, Jesus, from above,	248
Come sing to me of Heaven	296
Come sinners to the Gospel feast	60
Come thou all-inspiring Spirit	223
Come thou Almighty King	20
Come thou fount of every blessing	135
Come to Jesus, pensive mourner	75
Come ye disconsolate	124
Come, weary sinners, come	63
Come, ye sinners, poor and needy	52
Come ye that love the Lord	139
Commit thou all thy griefs	183
Dark was the night and cold the ground	48
Deepen the wounds thy hands have made	265
Delay not, delay not, O sinner draw near	50
Depth of mercy! can there be	101
Did Christ o'er sinners weep	83
Drooping souls no longer grieve	110
Equip me for the war	226
Eternal Sun of righteousness	123
Ever fainting with desire	252
Fade, fade each earthly joy	140
Father, at thy footstool see	24
Father, behold with gracious eye	15
Father, hear the blood of Jesus	88
Father, I dare believe	129
Father, I stretch my hands to thee	76

Father, if I may call thee so.................	78
Father of Jesus Christ, my Lord	111
Father of our dying Lord.....................	85
Father, Son and Holy Ghost...................	235
Father, supply my every need.................	185
Father, to thee, my soul I lift	21
Forever here my rest shall be................	232
Forever with the Lord........................	311
Fountain of life to all below................	23
From all that dwell below the skies	144
From every stormy wind that blows............	10
From the cros uplifted high..................	71
Gently Lord, O gently lead us................	212
Give me the wings of faith to rise...........	319
God is my strong salvation...................	104
God leadeth me; O blessed thought............	227
God of love who hearest prayer...............	24
God of my life, what just return.............	78
God of my salvation hear.....................	112
God's holy law transgressed..................	129
Grace, 'tis a charming sound.................	157
Gracious Spirit, Love divine.................	100
Great God, indulge my humble claim...........	108
Guide me, O thou great Jehovah...............	206
Hail, Sovreign Love, that first began........	165
Hail, thou once despised Jesus...............	160
Hail, to the Lords' anointed.................	168
Happy the souls to Jesus joined..............	318
Hark! my soul, it is the Lord................	72
Hark! the glad sound, the Saviour comes......	150
Hark! the Gospel news is sounding............	53
Hasten sinner to be wise.....................	43
Hast thou not heard of Gileads' balm.........	55
Hear the royal proclamation..................	57

Heavenly Father, I would wear	273
He wills that I should holy be	271
Help, Lord, to whom for help I fly	192
Help us to help each other, Lord	274
Here o'er the earth as a stranger I roam	198
Here we meet to part again	320
Ho! all ye hungry, starving souls	58
Ho! every one that thirsts, draw nigh	68
Holy and true, and righteous Lord	262
Holy Lamb, who thee receive	266
Holy Spirit, pity me	93
Hosanna to Jesus	178
How firm a foundation, ye saints	214
How happy every child of grace	316
How happy is the pilgrim's lot	283
How lost was my condition	171
How much of joy and comfort	201
How sweet and heavenly is the sight	182
How sweet the name of Jesus sounds	154
I'm bound for the land of the living	297
I'm a lonely traveller here	315
I'm but a stranger here	302
I'm glad salvation's free	173
I'm not ashamed to own my Lord,	218
I ask the gift of righteousness	256
I have sought round this verdant earth	176
I heard the voice of Jesus say	202
I know that my Redeemer lives, and	268
I know that my Redeemer lives! What	129
I lay my sins on Jesus	105
I lift mine eyes to thee	264
I long to behold him arrayed	303
I love thy kingdom, Lord	188
I'll praise my Maker while I've breath	172

I need thee, precious Jesus	130
I thirst, thou wounded Lamb of God	251
I want a principle within	209
I want thy life, thy purity	256
I want to live as one who knows	242
I want to live near Jesus	230
I would be thine, O take my heart	77
I would love Thee, heavenly Father	207
I would not live away	308
If thou impart thyself to me	260
In God we put our trust	234
In hope against all human hope	106
In life's joyous morning	50
In seasons of grief, to my God	27
In the Christian's home in glory	286
In the cross of Christ I glory	206
In thy name, O Lord, assembling	26
Jerusalem, my happy home	291
Jesus, accept the praise	323
Jesus, all-atoning Lamb	276
Jesus, and shall it ever be	186
Jesus comes with all his grace	258
Jesus died on Calvary's mountain	141
Jesus engrave it on my heart	99
Jesus hath died that I might live	257
Jesus, I love thy charming name	164
Jesus, I my cross have taken	236
Jesus, let thy pitying eye	102
Jesus, lover of my soul	80
Jesus my all to Heaven is gone	238
Jesus, my life, thyself apply	272
Jesus, our best beloved friend	263
Jesus, plant and root in me	267
Jesus, Redeemer, Saviour, Lord	106

Jesus, shall I never be	220
Jesus, the gift divine, I know	185
Jesus, the Lamb of God hath bled	124
Jesus the Lord of glory died	154
Jesus, the name high over all	142
Jesus, the sinner's friend, to thee	94
Jesus, the sinner's rest thou art	264
Jesus, thine all-victorious love	255
Jesus, thy blood and righteousness	132
Jesus, to thee I now can fly	107
Jesus, united by thy grace	182
Jesus, we look to thee	16
Join all the glorious names	143
Joy to the world! the Lord is come	150
Joyfully, joyfully, onward I move	199
Just as I am, without one plea	116
Just as thou art without one trace	69
Let Earth and Heaven agree	177
Let Him to whom we now belong	233
Let me go where saints are going	301
Let the world their virtues boast	131
Let worldly minds the world pursue	260
Lift your eyes of faith and see	305
Listen to the gentle promptings	45
Live on the field of battle	220
Lo! on a narrow neck of land	44
Lo! round the throne a glorious band	308
Lord, at thy feet we sinners lie	82
Lord, dismiss us with thy blessing	324
Lord, fill me with an humble fear	229
Lord, God, the Holy Ghost	18
Lord, how secure and blest are they	187
Lord, I am thine, entirely thine	249
Lord, I approach the mercy seat	96

INDEX.

Lord, I believe a rest remains	261
Lord, I despair myself to heal	95
Lord, we come before thee now	8
Lord, when we bend before thy throne	14
Lord, with glowing heart I'd praise thee	170
Love divine, all love excelling	253
Mercy alone can meet my case	114
Mid scenes of confusion and creature	216
Must Jesus bear the cross alone	226
My days are gliding swiftly by	300
My faith looks up to thee	117
My feet are weary with the march	280
My God, I am thine, what a comfort	178
My God, my God, to thee I cry	96
My God, my life, my love	147
My God, the spring of all my joys	159
My heavenly home is bright and fair	294
My hope is built on nothing less	132
My hope, my all, my Saviour, thou	186
My latest sun is sinking fast	310
My soul be on thy guard	225
My soul's full of glory	167
My span of life will soon be done	211
Nearer my God to thee	196
Not what these hands have done	134
Now e'en now I yield	269
Now I have found the ground	113
Now is the accepted time	74
Now the Saviour standeth pleading	34
O bless the Lord, my soul	146
O, Christian, are you ready now	304
O, Christian, walk carefully, danger is near	213
O come and dwell in me	245
O could I lose myself in thee	91

O could I speak the matchless	172
O fly mourning sinner, saith Jesus	66
O for a closer walk with God	82
O for a faith that will not shrink	133
O for a glance of heavenly day	79
O for a heart to praise my God	232
O for a thousand tongues to sing	158
O glorious hope of perfect love	246
O God, most merciful and true	248
O God, what offering shall I give	241
O happy day that fixed my choice	145
O how happy are they	174
O Jesus, at thy feet we wait	268
O Lamb of God still keep me	194
O land of rest for thee I sigh	291
O Lord, thy work revive	17
O love divine, how sweet thou art	247
O might I this moment cease	277
O Saviour, welcome to my heart	269
O say not, I will yet delay	49
O sinner, on the brink of death	36
O Sun of righteousness, arise	97
O tell me no more of this world's	217
O that I could repent	98
O that I could revere	98
O there is a fountain that never	73
O thou Exalted Son of God	270
O thou God of my salvation	152
O thou, in whose presence, my soul takes	148
O thou, our Saviour, Brother, Friend	11
O thou that hearest prayer	19
O thou, to whose all-searching sight	250
O thou, who camest from above	25
O thou, who hast our sorrows borne	84

O 'tis delight without alloy	151
O turn ye, O turn ye, for why will	51
O what amazing words of grace	54
O what shall I do my Saviour to praise	149
O when shall I see Jesus	278
O when shall we sweetly remove	317
O who'll stand up for Jesus	200
O who's like my Saviour	166
O ye young, ye gay, ye proud	44
Of Him who did salvation bring	144
On Jordan's stormy banks I stand	281
One sweetly solemn thought	299
Palms of glory, raiment white	295
Praise God, from whom all blessings	324
Prayer is appointed to convey	10
Prayer is the soul's sincere desire	23
Prince of Peace, control my will	259
Prostrate at Jesus' feet	92
Rejoice, the Lord is King	161
Rest for my soul I long to find	239
Return, O wanderer, return, and	54
Return, O wanderer, return	61
Rock of ages cleft for me	119
Salvation, O the joyful sound	151
Saviour of the sin-sick soul	258
Saviour, when in dust to thee	13
Saviour, while my heart is tender	237
See Jesus, thy disciples see	23
Shall I for fear of feeble man	228
Show pity Lord, O Lord forgive	90
Sinner go, will you go	67
Sinners, Jesus died for you	72
Sinners, obey the Gospel word	60
Sinners, the voice of God regard	38

Sinners, this solemn truth regard	29
Sinners turn, while God is near	41
Sinners turn, why will you die	40
Son of God, thy blessing grant	9
Sov'reign ruler, Lord of all	160
Spirit of life, and light, and love	21
Stand up for Jesus, all who lead	195
Stand up, stand up for Jesus	206
Stay thou insulted Spirit, stay	90
Still nigh me, O my Saviour, stand	191
Stop, poor sinners, and look yonder	35
Stop, poor sinners, stop and think	42
Sweet hour of prayer	12
Sweet the moments rich in blessing	210
Sweet rivers of redeeming love	284
Take my heart, O Father, take it	88
That awful day will surely come	37
The day of wrath that dreadful day	32
The Lord is my Shepherd, how happy am I	166
The Lord is my Shepherd, no want shall	214
The Lord my Shepherd is	156
The praying Spirit breathe	16
The Spirit of our hearts	62
The thing my God doth hate	244
There is a beautiful world	314
There is fountain filled with blood	125
There is a happy land	285
There is a Heaven above the skies	287
There is a land of pure delight	280
There is a place where my hopes	298
There is an hour when I must part	47
There is no night in heaven	313
There is a Friend above all others	64
This is not my place of resting	319

This world can never give............................	28
Though I have grieved thy Spirit, Lord	89
Though troubles assail, and dangers affright........	181
Thou Lamb of God, for sinners slain	81
Thy loving Spirit, Lord alone.......................	262
To-day, if you will hear his voice..................	46
To-day, the Saviour calls...........................	62
To Father, Son and Holy Ghost.......................	322
To Jesus' name give thanks..........................	169
To thee, O my Saviour, to thee will I cling.........	216
Together let us sweetly live........................	322
Vain are all terrestrial pleasures..................	204
Vain, delusive world, adieu.........................	184
Vain man, thy fond pursuits forbear.................	39
Walk in the light, so shalt thou know...............	218
Weary souls that wander wide........................	65
We by his Spirit prove..............................	128
We go the way that leads to God	293
We have no outward righteousness....................	121
We know, by faith, we know..........................	211
We may spread our couch with roses	208
We're travelling home to Heaven above...............	70
We who in Christ believe............................	156
Welcome, welcome, dear Redeemer.....................	275
What is our calling's glorious hope.................	254
What! never speak one evil word.....................	239
When gathering clouds around I view.................	220
When I can read my title clear......................	224
When I survey the wondrous cross....................	228
When, my Saviour, shall I be........................	266
When shall I see the welcome hour...................	272
When shall thy love constrain.......................	92
When we hear the music ringing......................	279
Where are the dead? In Heaven or Hell...............	83
Wherewith, O Lord, shall I draw near................	94
While God invites how blessed the day...............	33
While we walk with God in white.....................	180
With joy we meditate the grace......................	114
With pitying eyes the prince of grace...............	155
Ye who know your sins forgiven......................	243
Ye wretched, starving poor..........................	74

www.ingramcontent.com/pod-product-compliance
Lightning Source LLC
Chambersburg PA
CBHW021152230426
43667CB00006B/353